fresh ITALIAN COOKING
FOR THE NEW GENERATION

fresh ITALIAN COOKING
FOR THE NEW GENERATION

100 FULL-FLAVORED VEGETARIAN DISHES THAT PROVE YOU CAN EAT PASTA AND BREAD WHILE STAYING SLIM

**ALEXANDRA
CASPERO LENZ**, R.D.
CREATOR OF DELISH KNOWLEDGE

PAGE STREET
PUBLISHING CO.

PAGE STREET
PUBLISHING CO.

First published in 2016 by

Page Street Publishing Co.

27 Congress Street, Suite 103

Salem, MA 01970

www.pagestreetpublishing.com

Distributed by Macmillan, sales in Canada by The Canadian Manda Group.

19 18 17 16   1 2 3 4 5

ISBN-13: 978-1-62414-260-4

ISBN-10: 1-62414-260-5

Library of Congress Control Number: 2015960296

Cover and book design by Page Street Publishing Co.

Photography by Jennifer Blume

Printed and bound in the United States

Page Street is proud to be a member of 1% for the Planet. Members donate one percent of their sales to one or more of the over 1,500 environmental and sustainability charities across the globe who participate in this program.

FOR MORMOR, FOR YOUR FEARLESSNESS AND SENSE OF
ADVENTURE INSIDE THE KITCHEN AND OUT.
I MISS YOU.

contents

HOMEMADE PASTA   162

THE BASICS   179

THE ITALIAN PANTRY   192

introduction

WHY ITALIANS DON'T GET FAT

I have always considered pasta to be one of life's greatest pleasures. It's healthy, versatile and always delicious. When the low-carb and Paleo crazes hit, I was saddened to see pasta being labeled as public enemy number one. How could my beloved pasta be responsible for so many of the claims against it? I had grown up in a household where pasta was king, eaten at least once a day and always promoted by my parents as one of the healthiest foods we could eat.

Somewhere along the way, pasta was assigned the stigma of being unhealthy, along the same lines as rice, bread and everything gluten-filled. Sure, these foods have calories, but can we please stop blaming carbs? The nutrition scientist in me knows that eating carbs alone doesn't equate with weight gain. There are so many factors to take into consideration, and pasta is only one of them. Pasta itself is nourishing, contains very little fat and, when consumed in moderation, is fairly low in calories. The truth is, portion size still matters. Any food consumed in large quantities is unhealthy, regardless of its carbohydrate content. A moderate-sized bowl of pasta won't make you gain weight; however, consistently eating an entire box of pasta might. If you've been avoiding grains for weight-loss purposes, I'm happy to report that it's possible to have your noodle and eat it too.

Most of the recipes in this book follow my nutrient-density approach to food. Or, as I like to call it, "the biggest bang for your calorie buck." The nutrient-density approach examines the quantity of nutrients you receive from a food, given the number of calories it contains. It's a simple way to balance nutrients with calories. Simply stated, we should emphasize foods in our diet that are rich in vitamins, minerals, phytochemicals and antioxidants, and low in calories. Ironically, this is the way I grew up eating, I just didn't have a name for it. Yes, we ate pasta daily, but it was rarely in excess. Our plates were filled with in-season vegetables, salads, lean proteins and pasta. I learned to find satisfaction in healthy portions; we ate until we were satisfied, not stuffed.

Nutrient density works as a weight-loss/weight-management tool because it doesn't feel as restrictive as other weight-loss approaches. You still get to enjoy your favorite foods by dressing them up with nutrient-dense ingredients. Even as a registered dietitian, I despise the idea of counting calories. Instead, I value nutrients. My recipes are colorful, packed with nutrients and, most importantly, delicious.

THE PLANT-BASED TABLE

In high school and college, I dabbled with the idea of vegetarianism. I was never a huge fan of meat and tended to naturally favor bowls of pasta and salads over roasted chicken and steak. I ate meat because I thought I had to, because it contained vital nutrients essential to my health. As I started to learn more about nutrition, I realized that I could get all of my nutrients in plants—without meat! Of course in those days, we still thought that plant proteins had to be combined for optimal health. I remember tracking meals in my planner, making sure that I checked the box for each of the required amino acid groups. Well, nutrition science has come a long way since then. Thanks to an abundance of research that demonstrates the health and environmental benefits of a plant-based diet, we now know it's in everyone's best interest to consume fewer animal products and more vegetables, fruits and grains.

The saying "let food be thy medicine and medicine be thy food" has never been more appropriate. An estimated 70 percent of all diseases, including one-third of all cancers, are related to diet. A plant-based diet reduces the risk for chronic diseases and conditions such as obesity, coronary artery disease, high blood pressure, diabetes and certain types of cancer, including colon, breast, prostate, stomach, lung and esophageal. The good news is that including meatless meals even a few times a week has significant benefits. Therefore, this book is for everyone: vegetarians, vegans and die-hard carnivores. My goal is to show that plant-based Italian food is satisfying, wholesome and mouth-watering.

THE ITALIAN TABLE

Most of these recipes are 50-plus years in the making. They are adaptions from the recipes that were passed down from both my mother and grandmother. These are dishes that I grew up eating and now feed to my own family. I wanted to write this book as a way of sharing with you the vital role that pasta has played in my family. When we get together, there is almost always a bowl of pasta in the middle of the table, ready to be lingered over with hours of conversation.

In discussing the virtues of Italian cuisine, I would be remiss not to include a conversation around the slow-food culture of the Italian table. Food is to be savored, not rushed. Even on busy weeknights, our family dinners were typically two-course affairs—pasta or soup as a starter, meat or fish as an optional second, and always a green salad to finish. As a kid, I hated having such drawn-out meals, but as an adult, there's nothing I value more than quality family time around the table. The slow-food concept adds to the health benefits of Italian food. There is a huge difference in how your body processes a meal that was devoured versus one that was leisurely enjoyed. A slower approach to eating leads to better digestion, satisfaction and a greater ability to realize how much food your body really needs. When we hurry through meals, we end up eating much more than we need, leading to indigestion, guilt and, eventually, weight gain. I know it's not realistic to expect everyone to set aside several hours for dinner each evening—some days I can barely muster 30 minutes for my family. However, slowing down is key to a happy weight and personal well-being. Taking your time to eat and savor food is one of the most powerful things you can do for increased happiness and health. Life is stressful enough, eating doesn't have to be.

"A good cook knows it's not what's on the table that matters, it's what is in the chairs." My mom has that quote plastered on the fridge, and I think it's the best reminder for what yummy food really is: It's an opportunity to spend quality time with friends and family around the table. I love Italian food because there's little pretentiousness, and it's nearly foolproof to create. The cuisine is rustic, centered around ripe, in-season produce and incorporates flavorful sauces with drizzles of quality olive oil and cheese. My recipes are adaptations of generations of cooks. They're simple, healthy and nourishing to both the body and the soul. I hope these recipes not only feed your family, but bring your family closer together.

Buon appetito!

A NOTE ON VEGAN OPTIONS: All of the recipes in this cookbook are vegetarian, and many can be made vegan with a few substitions. Whenever possible, I've included directions for vegan versions at the bottom of the recipe.

light and lean weeknight pasta

These are the recipes I turn to almost daily. They're fast, simple dishes that highlight in-season produce. Pasta, vegetables and a sprinkle of herbs and grated cheese create a filling meal and further prove that delicious food doesn't have to be complicated. My Pasta Checca with Burrata (page 40) is probably one of the quickest dishes you can prepare, while Butternut Mac and Cheese (page 25) will quickly become your favorite stovetop version.

All of these recipes are paired with plenty of vegetables, allowing you to enjoy a healthy serving of pasta and vegetables in one dish. If you're looking for fast and fresh, you'll find it here.

GNOCCHI WITH FRESH CORN AND ZUCCHINI SAUCE

— SERVES 4 —

To me, this dish is a celebration of summer. I make it almost weekly when my basil and zucchini plants are overflowing. Freshly shucked corn, zucchini and lots of fresh basil transform ordinary gnocchi into this height-of-summer staple. I know that removing corn kernels can be a pain, but don't be tempted to swap in frozen corn instead. The secret to this sauce is the lightly browned butter combined with silky, fresh corn and Parmesan cheese. While gnocchi is my favorite pasta to use here, you can substitute in cooked tortellini or penne, or forgo the pasta altogether for a vegetable side dish.

FRESH CORN
AND ZUCCHINI SAUCE

¼ cup (60 g) butter

½ cup (45 g) white or yellow onion, finely diced

Salt and freshly ground black pepper

2 cloves garlic, chopped

4 cups (460 g) zucchini (about 3 zucchini), diced

2½ cups (450 g) fresh corn kernels (about 3 ears corn)

1 tsp dried oregano

1 (17.5-oz [500-g]) package vacuum-packed gnocchi

½ cup (20 g) fresh basil, chopped

¼ cup (25 g) Parmesan cheese, freshly grated

Bring a large pot of salted water to a boil.

Heat the butter in a large skillet over medium-high heat until melted and slightly browned. Add the onion and cook until soft, about 3–5 minutes. Add in a generous pinch of salt and pepper. Add the garlic, zucchini, corn kernels and oregano. Cook for 5–8 minutes until soft. Season to taste with salt and pepper.

While the zucchini and corn are cooking, add the gnocchi to the boiling water and cook until gnocchi start to float to the top. As soon as the gnocchi float to the surface, scoop out and place in a large bowl. Add the cooked zucchini and corn mixture to the gnocchi. Stir in chopped basil leaves and Parmesan cheese.

VEGAN VERSION: Replace butter with non-dairy butter, same amount. Replace Parmesan cheese with Vegan Parmesan Cheese (page 182), same amount.

MEDITERRANEAN ZUCCHINI LINGUINE

— SERVES 6–8 —

Even though I will always love a big bowl of pasta, I was quickly suckered into the spiralized noodle trend, creating endless recipes out of zucchini and squash noodles. I loved the lighter take on my Italian favorites, and am using a similar technique for this dish. Since not everyone owns a spiralizer, this recipe calls for ribbons of zucchini quickly made with an old-fashioned vegetable peeler. Simply shave the zucchini into long, wide strips that resemble sheets of freshly made pasta. Of course, you could forgo the linguine entirely, but this recipe is a perfect example of the fact that pasta doesn't have to be indulgent to be delicious. By combining whole-wheat linguine and zucchini noodles, you save calories without sacrificing flavor. Since it's a crowd pleaser, I'm suggesting a 6 to 8 person serving size, but this dish can easily be halved or doubled, depending on who is coming for dinner. The sauce is just as effortless; briny and fresh thanks to the generous use of herbs, cherry tomatoes and kalamata olives.

3 medium zucchini

8 oz (225 g) linguine (whole-wheat if desired)

¼ cup (60 ml) extra virgin olive oil

1 pint (300 g) cherry tomatoes, halved

¼ tsp crushed red pepper flakes

Salt and freshly ground black pepper

4 garlic cloves, minced

¾ cup (100 g) kalamata olives, pitted and chopped

1 tbsp (15 ml) red wine vinegar

½ cup (25 g) fresh parsley leaves, chopped

½ cup (15 g) fresh basil, chopped

1 cup (115 g) feta cheese, crumbled

Using a vegetable peeler, shave the zucchini into long, wide strips. Place into a colander and set aside.

Bring a large pot of salted water to a boil. Add the linguine and cook until al dente. Drain, reserving ½ cup (188 ml) pasta water, and set aside.

Heat the olive oil over medium heat in a large saucepan. Add the cherry tomatoes, zucchini strips, crushed red pepper flakes and a pinch each of salt and pepper, and cook until soft, about 5 minutes. Stir in the minced garlic cloves, kalamata olives and red wine vinegar, and cook another minute. Add the linguine to the saucepan and stir to combine. If the mixture is too thick, add in 1–2 tablespoons (15–30 ml) of reserved pasta water to thin. You may not need the pasta water—it will depend on how watery your zucchini is.

Add the parsley, basil and feta cheese, and season to taste with salt and pepper. Mix well and serve immediately.

VEGAN VERSION: Omit the feta cheese.

BALSAMIC MUSHROOM PASTA

— SERVES 4 —

This pasta can be vegan or vegetarian, depending on if you want to use cashew cream or heavy cream. I love cashew cream and tend to use it in any recipe that calls for heavy cream. It's simple to make and only requires three ingredients plus a high-powered blender or food processor. Once you start making it, you may never stop. Since it keeps in the fridge for 3 to 4 days and frozen for up to 6 months, I almost always have a small container on hand to dress up pasta, grain bowls and salad dressings. If your blender or food processor is large, you may need to double the cashew recipe so that there is enough in the blender to make it creamy. If not, it will just get stuck on the underside of the blade. Once pureed, the cream should be creamy and very smooth.

CASHEW CREAM

¼ cup (35 g) raw cashews, soaked for at least 30 minutes

⅛ cup (30 ml) water

2 tsp (10 ml) fresh lemon juice

Salt

(Or, instead of Cashew Cream, ⅛ cup [30 ml] heavy cream)

8 oz (225 g) fettuccine

1 tbsp (15 ml) extra virgin olive oil

⅓ cup (60 g) shallot, finely diced

3 garlic cloves, minced

10 oz (285 g) baby portobello mushrooms, sliced

⅓ cup (80 ml) balsamic vinegar

2 tbsp (5 g) fresh parsley leaves, chopped

Salt and freshly ground black pepper

If not making Cashew Cream, skip this paragraph and begin with making the pasta. Place the cashews in a bowl and fill with water at least an inch (2.5 cm) above the cashews. Allow the cashews to soak for 30 minutes or up to overnight. Drain and rinse the cashews. Place the cashews, water, lemon juice and a pinch of salt in a high-powered blender or food processor. Blend until very creamy and smooth. Set aside.

Bring a large pot of salted water to a boil. Add the fettuccine and cook to al dente according to package directions. Drain and set aside.

Meanwhile, heat olive oil over medium heat in a large skillet. Add the shallots and garlic and cook for a few minutes until just softened.

Add the mushrooms to the shallots and garlic and cook until golden brown, about 5–8 minutes. Pour in the balsamic vinegar and scrape up all of the browned bits on the bottom of the skillet.

Remove the mushroom mix from the heat and stir in the reserved cashew cream or heavy cream. Add in the cooked fettuccine and toss to combine. Add in the parsley and season to taste with salt and pepper.

SPICY BROCCOLI RABE AND GEMELLI PASTA

— SERVES 4 —

I can't say enough good things about this simple dish. Growing up, the only way I would eat bitter broccoli rabe was with lots of grated Parmesan cheese and spicy crushed red pepper flakes. As I've gotten older, I appreciate the adult flavor, and seek it out over more readily available broccoli or broccolini.

As I've learned with my recipe testers, spicy is a variable. If you tend to prefer spicy food, start with ¾ teaspoon of crushed red pepper flakes and go from there. For a milder version, use a smaller pinch, roughly ¼ teaspoon to ½ teaspoon.

10 oz (285 g) gemelli pasta (about 2½ cups dried)

2 bunches broccoli rabe, cut into 2-inch (5-cm) pieces

4 tbsp (60 ml) extra virgin olive oil

½–¾ tsp crushed red pepper flakes, or to taste

4 garlic cloves, minced

1 (15.5-oz [435-g]) can chickpeas, rinsed and drained

Salt and freshly ground black pepper

⅓ cup (35 g) Parmesan cheese, freshly grated

Bring a large pot of salted water to a boil. Add the gemelli pasta and cook until al dente. Using a slotted spoon, remove the pasta and place in a large bowl. Remove ½ cup (118 ml) of the pasta cooking water and set aside.

Bring the remaining pasta water back to a boil and add the broccoli rabe. Cook for 2 minutes and then drain.

Heat a large skillet over medium-high heat. Add the oil and crushed red pepper flakes and cook for 30 seconds–1 minute until the crushed red pepper flakes are slightly toasted but not burnt. Reduce the heat to medium and stir in the garlic. Add the chickpeas, reserved broccoli rabe and a pinch each of salt and pepper. Cook until rabe is tender, about 3–4 minutes.

Add in the pasta to the skillet. If the pasta sticks together, add a little bit of reserved pasta water to thin the sauce. Stir in Parmesan cheese and serve immediately.

NOTE: If you can't find broccoli rabe, substitute broccolini or broccoli florets.

VEGAN VERSION: Replace Parmesan cheese with Vegan Parmesan Cheese (page 182), same amount.

PASTA ALLA NORMA

— SERVES 6–8 —

I love cooking with eggplant but despise the excess oil that's often needed to transform eggplant from bitter to meaty and rich. To cut down on the excess oil, I've roasted the eggplant instead of sautéing it. This technique keeps the rich, delicate flavor of the dish with a fraction of the calories. While it sounds similar, ricotta salata isn't the same as creamy ricotta; I often find it in well-stocked grocery stores in the specialty cheese section. If you have a hard time locating the salty, sheep's milk cheese, substitute with shaved Parmesan or feta cheese instead.

1½ lb (125 g) eggplant, cut into ½–¾-inch (1.5–2-cm) cubes

2 tbsp (30 ml) extra virgin olive oil, divided

1 (28-oz [795-g]) can crushed tomatoes

3 cloves garlic, chopped

¼ tsp crushed red pepper flakes, or to taste

1 tsp dried oregano

Salt and freshly ground black pepper

1 lb (455 g) penne pasta

½ cup (5 g) fresh basil leaves, chopped

½ cup (55 g) ricotta salata, grated

Preheat oven to 450°F (232°C).

Toss eggplant with 1 tablespoon (15 ml) olive oil and place on a baking sheet. Roast for 10–12 minutes or under tender, turning halfway through.

Place the remaining 1 tablespoon (15 ml) of olive oil in a large saucepan over medium heat. Add the crushed tomatoes, garlic, crushed red pepper flakes and oregano. Cook until hot, 10 minutes, stirring often so that the sauce doesn't stick to the bottom. Season with pepper and a pinch of salt. Add in the eggplant. Reduce heat to low and simmer while you make the pasta.

Bring a large pot of salted water to a boil. Add the penne and cook until just al dente. Drain.

Add the drained pasta to the eggplant and tomato sauce and stir together. I like to add my pasta when it's almost finished and then let it cook in the sauce for maximum flavor. Once the pasta is done, remove from heat and stir in basil. Garnish with ricotta salata and serve.

NOTE: I'm fairly lazy when it comes to peeling vegetables, so I leave the eggplant peel on. If you find eggplant with peel too bitter, feel free to peel the vegetable before cubing.

VEGAN VERSION: Omit the ricotta salata.

ROASTED VEGETABLE PASTA

— SERVES 6–8 —

One of my most beloved kitchen tools is my roasting pan. It's my preferred way for introducing vegetable dishes and my go-to when I don't know what to cook for dinner. Typically, I just cut up whatever vegetables I have lying around in the fridge, toss with olive oil, add salt and pepper and roast to perfection. A stir or two later and I am rewarded with caramelized bites of vegetables that encourage me to enjoy cup after cup. It was after one of these evenings that this recipe was born: roasted vegetables tossed with hot linguine, a quick tomato sauce and a little bit of cheese. It's simple and a must on days you want to eat healthy but don't feel like a salad.

Caramelized vegetables taste miles away from steamed or boiled so even if you don't think you love vegetables, you will love them in this dish. While roasting doesn't require much technique, here are my secrets to perfect vegetables every time. The vegetables should be cut into equal-sized pieces so they will cook at a relatively even rate. Similarly, they need to be spread in an even layer on a baking sheet, sometimes two, depending on how many vegetables you are roasting. If the vegetables are mounded on top of one another, they will steam in the pan and not roast. Lastly, make sure to stir them once or twice while cooking so the vegetables get nicely browned on all sides. From there, the possibilities are endless.

1 lb (455 g), zucchini, chopped into bite-sized pieces

1 red bell pepper, chopped into 1-inch (2.5-cm) pieces

1 bunch asparagus, trimmed and cut into 2-inch (5-cm) pieces

1 tbsp (15 ml) plus 1 tsp extra virgin olive oil, divided

¼ tsp plus ⅛ tsp crushed red pepper flakes

Salt and freshly ground black pepper

1 small white onion, diced

½ tsp dried oregano

3 garlic cloves, thinly sliced

1 (28-oz [825-g]) can crushed tomatoes

12 oz (340 g) linguine

½ cup (10 g) fresh basil leaves, chopped

¼ cup (25 g) Parmesan cheese, freshly grated, optional

Preheat the oven to 400°F (204°C).

Toss the zucchini, red bell pepper and asparagus with 1 tablespoon (15 ml) olive oil, ¼ teaspoon crushed red pepper flakes and a large pinch each of salt and pepper. Place in a single layer on a baking sheet and roast for 25–35 minutes until tender and slightly caramelized.

Heat 1 teaspoon of olive oil in a large non-stick skillet over medium heat. Add in the onion and cook until tender, about 5 minutes. Add another pinch of salt, pepper, ⅛ teaspoon crushed red pepper flakes, dried oregano and garlic cloves and cook another minute. Add the tomatoes, increasing heat to medium, and simmer for 15–20 minutes, stirring occasionally.

While the sauce is cooking, bring a large pot of salted water to a boil. Add the pasta to the boiling water and cook until al dente per package directions. Drain, reserving ½ cup (118 ml) pasta water.

Add the hot pasta to the skillet with the tomato sauce. Add the roasted vegetables and reserved cooking water to thin. Stir in the basil and Parmesan cheese, if using.

VEGAN VERSION: Forgo Parmesan cheese or replace with Vegan Parmesan (page 182), same amount.

BUTTERNUT MAC AND CHEESE

— SERVES 4 —

This is my answer to everyone's favorite blue box: creamy butternut squash puree with a hint of spice and cheddar cheese, tossed with hot shells. It's rich, flavorful and half the fat and calories of traditional mac and cheese. I could eat this as a main or side dish almost every night.

2 cups (800 g) elbow noodles or mini shells

2 cups (280 g) butternut squash, cubed

1 cup (240 ml) vegetable broth

1 garlic clove

⅛ tsp crushed red pepper flakes

⅛ tsp dried oregano

Freshly ground black pepper

¾ cup (85 g) shredded cheddar cheese

Salt

Bring a large pot of salted water to a boil. Add the noodles and cook until al dente according to package directions. Drain and set aside.

While the water is boiling, fill a saucepan with butternut squash and enough water to cover. Bring to a boil and simmer for 10–15 minutes until squash is fork tender. Drain.

Add the drained butternut squash to a high-powered blender or food processor, along with the vegetable broth, garlic clove, crushed red pepper flakes, oregano and a pinch of pepper. Puree until very smooth and creamy.

Place the butternut squash puree back in the saucepan and simmer over medium-low heat. Stir in the cheddar cheese until just melted. Add the cooked noodles and season to taste with salt and pepper. Depending on your vegetable broth, you may not need any additional salt. Enjoy hot!

PERFECT POMODORO SAUCE WITH CAPELLINI

— SERVES 6–8 —

One of the best restaurant meals of my life was in a tiny café on the outskirts of Florence. It was our first day in the city, and my husband and I were both exhausted from our long trip in. Luggage in tow, we stumbled inside a 10-seat restaurant and ordered from the daily chalkboard specials, unsure exactly what we were ordering since my Italian was very rusty. We were rewarded with the best bowl of pasta that either of us has ever had—a simple, rustic dish of spaghetti and fresh tomato sauce, unassuming yet mind-blowing. That meal is a constant reminder that when produce is fresh, you don't need much else.

Since the tomatoes are the undisputed stars of this dish, use the best that you can find. Like most produce-centered recipes, the better the tomato, the better the sauce. When tomatoes are blood red inside and so fresh you can smell them on the counter, it's time to make this sauce. To make things easier, I leave the skins on, but you are welcome to peel them if you prefer a smoother texture. Pull the pasta just before it's al dente, about one minute before the suggested cooking time. Finishing the pasta in the sauce infuses rich tomato flavor into every bite. Although it's tempting to do so, don't omit the pat of butter at the end. It really completes the sauce and pulls everything together.

POMODORO SAUCE

¼ cup (59 ml) extra virgin olive oil

4–5 cloves garlic, thinly sliced or minced

Salt and freshly ground black pepper

5 cups (900 g) tomatoes, chopped

1 tsp sugar

½ cup (5 g) fresh basil, roughly chopped

1 tbsp (15 g) butter

1 lb (450 g) capellini (angel hair pasta)

Heat the olive oil in a medium saucepan over medium heat. Add the garlic and a generous pinch of salt and pepper, stirring for 30 seconds–1 minute until fragrant but not burned. If you burn the garlic, remove it or else it will ruin the sauce. Add the chopped tomatoes and sugar and cook for 10–15 minutes until reduced and thick.

In the meantime, prepare your pasta. Bring a large pot of salted water to a boil. Add the pasta and cook until just undercooked, about 1 minute before the cooking time recommended in package directions. Drain, reserving ½ cup (118 ml) of pasta water.

Check on your sauce. If you like it chunky then leave it as is. I prefer a smoother sauce, so I pulse the sauce a few times using an immersion blender to make it thinner. Alternatively, you can puree a cup of sauce in a blender and add back to the tomatoes.

Add the basil and butter to the sauce. Toss in the pasta and let cook for 1–2 more minutes so the pasta finishes cooking in the sauce. If the pasta becomes too thick, add 1–2 tablespoons (15–30 ml) at a time of the reserved pasta water to thin.

VEGAN VERSION: Replace butter with non-dairy butter, same amount.

SUN-DRIED TOMATO AND GOAT CHEESE CAPELLINI

— SERVES 4 —

This pasta makes generous use of reserved pasta water, melting goat cheese crumbles into the hot pasta to create an indulgent pasta dish with only a fraction of the usual amount of cheese. The use of sun-dried tomatoes means you can enjoy this pasta all year long. I purchase the dried slivers, not the tomatoes packed in olive oil, to save even more calories.

8 oz (225 g) capellini (angel hair pasta)

1 tbsp (15 ml) extra virgin olive oil

1 white or yellow onion, chopped

4 garlic cloves, minced

¾ cup (85 g) sun-dried tomatoes, chopped

1 cup (240 ml) dry white wine

½ tsp sea salt, or to taste

¼ tsp freshly ground black pepper

¼ tsp crushed red pepper flakes

3 oz (85 g) goat cheese

⅛ cup (5 g) fresh parsley leaves, chopped

Bring a large pot of salted water to a boil. Add the capellini and cook until al dente according to package directions. Drain, reserving 1 cup (237 ml) pasta water.

While the water is boiling, heat the olive oil in a large skillet over medium heat. Add the onion and garlic and cook until just tender, about 3–4 minutes. Add in the sun-dried tomatoes, white wine, salt, pepper and crushed red pepper flakes and simmer until liquid is reduced by half.

Add the cooked capellini to the skillet and dot with goat cheese. Add in ½ cup (118 ml) of the reserved pasta water and toss together to melt the goat cheese into the pasta. Sauce should be thin and creamy—add in more pasta water if needed. Season to taste with salt and pepper and stir in the parsley. Serve immediately.

*See photo on page 12.

CASARECCE WITH LEMON PESTO AND VEGETABLES

— SERVES 4 —

Casarecce ("homemade") is a short pasta that looks like a scroll, twisted to capture every drop of the accompanying sauce. If you can't find caserecce, use any other short pasta like gemelli or penne. Prepared pesto brands vary widely in both flavor and nutrition. The prepared, refrigerated options are typically better than those found in the aisles.

Stirring in the splash of lemon juice completes this dish. It brightens the pesto and provides just a hint of tartness. In fact, a little bit of acid (fresh citrus or vinegar) at the end of cooking can completely transform even the most ho-hum of meals. It's a tip I picked up from my chef friends and what I turn to whenever I think something is missing. Try it and prepare to be amazed!

8 oz (227 g) casarecce pasta or other short pasta such as gemelli or penne

1 tbsp (15 ml) extra virgin olive oil

3 cups (273 g) broccoli florets

1 pint (300 g) cherry tomatoes, halved

½ tsp salt, or to taste

¼ tsp freshly ground black pepper

¼ tsp crushed red pepper flakes

⅛ cup (30 ml) fresh lemon juice

½ cup (120 ml) prepared pesto

Salt

¼ cup (25 g) Parmesan cheese, freshly grated

Bring a large pot of salted water to a boil. Add the casarecce and cook until al dente according to package directions. Drain, reserving ½ cup (118 ml) pasta water and set aside.

While the water is boiling, heat the olive oil in a large skillet over medium heat. Add the broccoli, cherry tomatoes, salt, pepper and crushed red pepper flakes. Cook for 10–12 minutes until broccoli is tender and tomatoes are soft. Remove from heat and stir in the cooked pasta, lemon juice and prepared pesto. Stir to combine. If the sauce is too thick, add in some of the reserved pasta water. Season to taste with salt and pepper and stir in the Parmesan cheese.

VEGAN VERSION: Replace Parmesan cheese with Vegan Parmesan Cheese (page 182), same amount.

CREAMY SUN-DRIED TOMATO BOW TIES

— SERVES 6–8 —

On my first trip to Italy, I made the mistake of only taking a carry-on bag with me. Great for navigating through tiny back streets and trains, not so great for bringing delicious souvenirs back with me. The next time I was prepared, bringing along a foldable bag inside of my suitcase to load up with dried pastas, olive oil, wine, limoncello and bags of sun-dried tomatoes. While those goodies are long gone, I will forever associate sun-dried tomatoes with those gifts from Italy and the endless bowls of this pasta that I made with them. The concentrated sun-dried tomato flavor gives a richness to this dish that could never be achieved with fresh tomatoes. For an extra chewy bite, I mix in a handful of slivered sun-dried tomatoes to the finished cream sauce.

If you're new to cashew cream, this is a great beginner's recipe to start off with. The trick is soaking the cashews for at least one hour, preferably longer, so they are easier to blend into a thick and creamy sauce. To cut down on overall calories, I'm combining both raw cashews and cauliflower to create a silky sauce to be tossed with hot bow ties, basil and sun-dried tomatoes.

⅓ cup (50 g) raw cashews, soaked at least 1 hour

1 tsp extra virgin olive oil

½ cup (45 g) white or yellow onion, chopped

3 cloves garlic, chopped

2 cups (25 g) cauliflower florets (about ½ head)

¼ tsp dried oregano

¼ tsp crushed red pepper flakes, or to taste

1 cup (236 ml) water

1 cup (236 ml) soy milk (or milk of choice)

⅔ cup (70 g) sun-dried tomatoes, chopped, divided

Salt and freshly ground black pepper

1 lb (455 g) farfalle pasta

¾ cup (20 g) fresh basil, finely chopped

Bring a large pot of salted water to a boil.

Drain the cashews and rinse well. Set aside.

Heat olive oil over medium heat in a large, nonstick skillet. Add the onion and cook until soft, about 5 minutes. Stir in the garlic and add the cauliflower florets, oregano and crushed red pepper flakes. Cook, stirring often, until florets are slightly soft. Remove from heat and place in a high-powered blender along with the drained cashews, water, soy milk, ⅓ cup (35 g) sun-dried tomatoes and a pinch each of salt and pepper. Puree until very smooth and creamy. Depending on the power of the blender, this may take up to 5 minutes. It should have the consistency of a cream sauce. If it's too thick, add a bit more water or milk.

While you puree the sauce, add the farfalle to the boiling water and cook until al dente. Drain, reserving 1 cup (237 ml) pasta water.

Toss the cooked pasta with the tomato cream sauce and remaining ⅓ cup (35 g) sun-dried tomatoes. If the sauce it too thick, thin with remaining pasta water. Stir in chopped basil and serve immediately.

SPAGHETTI SQUASH PASTA
WITH WALNUT BROWN BUTTER SAUCE

— SERVES 4 —

I know spaghetti squash is typically used to replace pasta altogether, but I like combining the two to create a healthy, nutrient-dense main dish. The secret to this sauce is removing as much water as possible from the cooked spaghetti squash. After removing the spaghetti-like strands from the cooked squash, place in a colander over the sink and gently squeeze strands to remove excess water.

Once I start making this sauce, I have to remind myself that I don't need to put brown butter on everything! There is honestly nothing like it; earthy, caramelized with just a hint of smoke. Toss with squash, pasta and walnut pieces for crunch, and dinner is served.

1 large spaghetti squash

4 oz (115 g) capellini (angel hair pasta) or thin spaghetti

¼ cup (60 g) unsalted butter

10–12 fresh sage leaves

½ cup (80 g) walnuts, chopped

¼ tsp crushed red pepper flakes

Salt and freshly ground black pepper

⅓ cup (35 g) Parmesan cheese, freshly grated

Preheat the oven to 350°F (176°C).

Halve the spaghetti squash. Remove the seeds and place facedown in a rimmed baking dish and cover with 2–3 inches (5–7.5 cm) of water so that the top of the halves are covered. Bake until fork tender, about 35–45 minutes, depending on the size of the squash. Remove from the oven and shred into spaghetti-like strands. Place in a colander to drain excess water.

While the squash is cooking, bring a large pot of water to a boil. Cook pasta until al dente, according to package directions. Drain, reserving ½ cup (118 ml) of pasta water.

Meanwhile, make the sauce. Heat the butter in a large skillet over medium-low heat until toasted and golden brown, about 5–10 minutes. Add in the sage leaves and fry until crispy. Remove the leaves from skillet, finely chop and set aside.

Increase the heat to medium and place the walnuts into the brown butter skillet for 30 seconds until just toasted. Add the crushed red pepper flakes and spaghetti squash, and cook until heated through, 8–10 minutes. Season to taste with salt and pepper.

Add in the pasta and a bit of the reserved pasta water to thin. Stir in the Parmesan cheese and the fried sage.

POPEYE'S SPAGHETTI WITH MUSHROOMS

— SERVES 4 —

This is how I most often enjoy pasta—a simple sauté of vegetables in a light white wine sauce with spaghetti. It's modest, guiltless and ready in less than 20 minutes.

8 oz (225 g) spaghetti or capellini (angel hair pasta)

1 tbsp (15 ml) extra virgin olive oil

1 pint (285 g) white or cremini mushrooms, thinly sliced

Salt and freshly ground black pepper

1 small white or yellow onion, finely chopped

3 garlic cloves, minced

8 oz (225 g) baby spinach leaves

¼ tsp crushed red pepper flakes

½ cup (120 ml) white wine

1 cup (240 ml) vegetable broth, low-sodium if desired

¼ cup (25 g) Parmesan cheese, freshly grated

Bring a large pot of salted water to a boil. Cook the pasta to al dente according to package directions. Drain and set aside.

While the pasta is cooking, make the sauce. Heat olive oil in a large skillet over medium heat. Add the mushrooms and sauté until golden brown, about 5 minutes. Stir in a pinch each of salt and pepper.

Add the onions and cook another 5 minutes until the onions are translucent and cooked through. Stir in the garlic and spinach and cook until the spinach has just wilted. Add in the crushed red pepper flakes and the white wine and cook until reduced by ⅔, stirring occasionally.

Add in the broth and cook for another 5 minutes, then stir in the Parmesan cheese. Add the cooked pasta to the sauce and cook together an additional minute. Season to taste with salt and pepper.

VEGAN VERSION: Replace Parmesan cheese with Vegan Parmesan Cheese (page 182), same amount.

LINGUINE WITH BUTTERNUT SQUASH AND GOAT CHEESE

— SERVES 4 —

I know, the combination sounds a little off, but trust me when I say that roasted butternut squash pairs beautifully with creamy goat cheese. I was inspired to create this pasta after trying a similar crostini in New Zealand last winter. Toasted baguette, local goat cheese and the most fantastic butternut squash puree. I cancelled my dinner order in favor of another order of those crostini. The moment I got home, I wanted to re-create the medley in a linguine dinner.

While it's nothing my grandmother would do, I love the way goat cheese warms and melts into hot pasta. It's a sauce without having to make an actual sauce. Simply toss with roasted squash and spinach; the entire dish is a showstopper for any fall event.

8 oz (225 g) linguine

1 tbsp (15 ml) extra virgin olive oil

3 cups (390 g) butternut squash, finely cubed

1 small white or yellow onion, sliced

3 cloves garlic, crushed

1 tsp dried oregano

¼ tsp crushed red pepper flakes

Salt and freshly ground black pepper

2 large handfuls (80 g) baby spinach leaves

¼ cup (30 g) goat cheese, divided

Bring a large pot of salted water to a boil. Add the linguine and cook until al dente according to package directions. Drain, reserving 1 cup (237 ml) of cooking liquid.

Meanwhile, heat olive oil in a large saucepan over medium heat. Add the butternut squash and cook for 10–15 minutes, stirring often, until tender. Add onion, garlic, oregano, crushed red pepper flakes and a pinch each of salt and pepper, and cook for another 5 minutes until onions are soft and fragrant. Add spinach, ⅛ cup (15 g) of the goat cheese, cooked fettuccine and ⅓ cup (78 ml) reserved cooking liquid, and toss to combine. If too thick, add in a little more pasta water, 1 tablespoon (15 ml) at a time.

Season to taste and serve topped with remaining ⅛ cup (15 g) goat cheese.

LEMON AND ASPARAGUS SPAGHETTI

— SERVES 4 —

Lemon lovers, this pasta is for you. I always have a bowl of fresh lemons on the counter, as a small squirt of fresh juice is the perfect way to finish and brighten just about any dish. This dish is my take on Spaghetti al Limone (spaghetti with lemon sauce), adding in spinach and asparagus for extra nutrition while keeping the refreshing lemon flavor.

To me, there's no such thing as too much lemon, but if you are nervous about the idea of lemon in your pasta, start with ⅛ cup (30 ml) of fresh juice and go from there. You can always add more or drizzle fresh lemon juice directly onto the pasta after plating.

8 oz (½ lb [225 g]) spaghetti or capellini (angel hair pasta)

2 tbsp (30 g) unsalted butter

2 tbsp (30 ml) extra virgin olive oil

1 bunch asparagus, cut into 1-inch (2.5-cm) pieces

Salt and freshly ground black pepper

2 cloves garlic, minced

1 large lemon, juiced and zested (about ¼ cup [59 ml] juice), plus extra juice for garnish

4 cups (105 g) baby spinach leaves

¼ cup (60 ml) heavy cream

¼ cup (25 g) Parmesan cheese, freshly grated, plus extra for garnish

¼ cup (5 g) fresh flat-leaf parsley leaves, chopped, plus extra for garnish

Bring a large pot of salted water to a boil over medium heat. Add the pasta and cook until al dente per package directions. Drain, reserving ½ cup (118 ml) pasta water.

Meanwhile, heat the butter over medium-high heat in a large skillet until melted. Add in the olive oil, asparagus and a small pinch each of salt and pepper, and cook until asparagus is bright green and fork tender.

Add in the garlic, lemon juice, lemon zest and spinach leaves, and cook until spinach just wilts. Add in the pasta and ¼ cup (59 ml) of the pasta water. Reduce heat to low and cook for a minute or two to form a sauce with the vegetables and pasta.

Turn off heat and slowly add in the heavy cream, a pinch each of salt and pepper, and Parmesan cheese, if using. If the pasta is too thick, add in more of the reserved pasta water to thin. Stir in parsley and serve.

Garnish with extra parsley, Parmesan cheese and a fresh squeeze of lemon juice, if desired.

VEGAN VERSION: Replaced butter with non-dairy butter, same amount. Replace heavy cream with ⅓ cup (78 ml) Cashew Cream (page 184). Replace Parmesan cheese with Vegan Parmesan Cheese (page 182), same amount.

EASY BRUSSELS SPROUTS PENNE

— SERVES 4 —

The key to this easy recipe is using a hot skillet with enough olive oil and salt to crisp the thinly sliced Brussels sprouts like potato chips. Charred and crispy, these are unlike any Brussels sprouts I had growing up. Even those who swear they don't love Brussels sprouts will enjoy them here. Out are the mushy, boiled sprouts and in are golden-brown, snack-worthy sprout leaves tossed with mushrooms, penne and plenty of Parmesan cheese. To speed up prep, I use my food processor fitted with a slicing blade to thinly slice the Brussels sprouts in under a minute.

8 oz (½ lb [230 g]) penne pasta

2 tbsp (30 ml) extra virgin olive oil, divided

1 jalapeño, thinly sliced

6 garlic cloves, minced

8 oz (225 g) mushrooms, sliced

8 oz (225 g) Brussels sprouts, thinly sliced

½ tsp Italian seasoning

¼ tsp crushed red pepper flakes

½ tsp salt, or to taste

¼ tsp freshly ground black pepper, or to taste

2 tbsp (30 ml) fresh lemon juice

¼ cup (25 g) Parmesan cheese, freshly grated

Bring large pot of salted water to a boil. Add the penne and cook until pasta is just al dente according to package directions. Drain and set aside.

Meanwhile, heat large cast-iron or sauté pan over medium-high heat and add 1 tablespoon (15 ml) olive oil. Add the sliced jalapeño and garlic cloves and cook for 30 seconds or until just fragrant. Add in the sliced mushrooms and cook until lightly browned, about 5 minutes. Add the remaining 1 tablespoon (15 ml) olive oil, Brussels sprouts, Italian seasoning, crushed red pepper flakes and the salt and pepper, and sauté until sprouts start to soften, then crisp, about 4–5 minutes. Gently spread sprouts mixture around in the pan and press down to flatten. Let sear for a minute, then stir it up and repeat. This helps brown the sprouts and make them crispy. Depending on the size of your pan, you may need to cook them in batches. You are aiming for crispy leaves, not steamed ones.

Add the cooked penne to the pan and toss until everything is well mixed. Stir in lemon juice and Parmesan cheese, and serve.

VEGAN VERSION: Replace Parmesan cheese with Vegan Parmesan Cheese (page 182), same amount.

ARTICHOKE RISOTTO WITH ORZO

— SERVES 4–6 —

Whenever I am under the weather, I turn to my favorite comfort meal—hot orzo tossed with a little butter and freshly grated Parmesan cheese. It's creamy, satisfying and so easy. This is my adult version of that dish, adding in tomatoes, peas and artichokes and keeping the satisfying bite of melted Parmesan cheese. For convenience, I rely on frozen versions of artichokes and peas. While you are welcome to use fresh, I call for the thawed, frozen version to cut down on prep. I prefer frozen to canned, but those will also work in a pinch. The key to using frozen hearts is that they must be thawed and then drained of any excess moisture. Otherwise, you risk adding excess water to whatever you are cooking,

1 tsp extra virgin olive oil

1 cup (115 g) onion, chopped

2 garlic cloves, chopped

5 cups (1.2 L) vegetable broth

1 cup (170 g) orzo

1 cup (180 g) tomatoes, chopped

6 oz (170 g) frozen artichokes, thawed and chopped

½ cup (80 g) frozen sweet peas, thawed

½ cup (5 g) fresh basil leaves, chopped

⅛ tsp crushed red pepper flakes

¼ cup (25 g) Parmesan cheese, freshly grated

Salt and freshly ground black pepper to taste

Heat the olive oil in a medium saucepan over medium heat. Add in the onion and garlic and cook until translucent, about 6–8 minutes.

While the onion is cooking, heat the broth in a separate pot over medium-low heat.

Add the orzo to the onion saucepan and stir to lightly toast, about 30 seconds–1 minute. Add in one ladle (about ¼–½ cup [59–118 ml]) of vegetable broth to the orzo and stir until liquid is almost completely absorbed. Continue to add the broth, one ladle at a time, until orzo is slightly tender but still firm, about 15 minutes. Add in the tomatoes, artichokes and peas and stir together. Continue adding the vegetable broth, one ladle at a time, until orzo is creamy and cooked through. You may not need all of the liquid.

Stir in the basil leaves, crushed red pepper flakes, Parmesan cheese, and salt and pepper. Depending on your vegetable broth, you may not need any additional salt.

VEGAN VERSION: Replace Parmesan cheese with Vegan Parmesan Cheese (page 182), same amount.

PASTA CHECCA WITH BURRATA

— SERVES 4 —

Pasta alla Checca! This no-cook pasta sauce is perfect for hot summer nights when you don't want to spend much time in the kitchen. Since it's a no-cook fresh tomato sauce, use the best tomatoes you can find. The fresher the tomato, the sweeter the sauce. Of course, you can serve the bright checca sauce with just pasta, but I can't help but put a spoonful or two of luscious burrata on top.

To serve, place the tossed pasta and sauce on a platter and dollop with fresh burrata.
If you can't find burrata, substitute fresh buffalo mozzarella.

8 oz (225 g) capellini (angel hair pasta)

4 scallions, white and pale green parts only, coarsely chopped

3 garlic cloves, chopped

3 small tomatoes

½ cup (5 g) fresh basil leaves, whole, plus extra torn leaves for garnish

1 tbsp (15 ml) extra virgin olive oil

¼ cup (25 g) Parmesan cheese, freshly grated

Salt and freshly ground black pepper to taste

4 oz (115 g) burrata cheese

Cook the pasta in a large pot of boiling salted water until al dente, tender but still firm to the bite, stirring often, about 8 minutes.

Meanwhile, combine the scallions, garlic cloves, tomatoes, basil leaves, olive oil and Parmesan cheese in a food processor. Pulse just until the tomatoes are very coarsely chopped but not pureed.

Drain the pasta, reserving ½ cup (118 ml) of the pasta water. Toss the pasta with the tomato mixture in a large bowl. If the pasta looks dry, add in some of the pasta water to thin. Season to taste with salt and pepper.

Place on a serving platter and dot with burrata. Garnish with torn basil leaves and serve immediately.

PASTA ALLA PUTTANESCA

— SERVES 4 —

This is my mom's signature pasta dish, a fact my sisters and I liked to tease her about after we discovered the sauce's namesake. Puttanesca means "relating to a prostitute." It was supposedly first created by ladies of the night who had little time to cook in between clients. Jokes aside, this is a fast weeknight pasta sauce that will soon become a favorite in your house—briny, acidic and bright. Everyone I make this dish for instantly falls in love with the simple tomato, olive and caper pairing. Though the sauce is traditionally made with anchovies, I'm subbing in a little olive and caper juice for that salty taste without the fish.

PUTTANESCA SAUCE

3 cloves garlic, minced

½ cup (90 g) kalamata olives, chopped

1 tbsp (15 ml) olive brine (juice from jar of olives)

1 (28-oz [795-g]) can diced tomatoes with juice

⅓ cup (60 g) capers

1 tbsp (15 ml) caper brine (juice from jar of capers)

¼ tsp crushed red pepper flakes

8 oz (225 g) spaghetti, whole wheat if preferred

½ cup (15 g) fresh parsley leaves, chopped

Combine the garlic, olives, olive brine, diced tomatoes with juice, capers, caper brine and crushed red pepper flakes together in a medium saucepan over medium heat. Simmer for 20 minutes while pasta is cooking.

Meanwhile, bring a large pot of salted water to a boil. Add the spaghetti and cook until al dente according to package directions. Drain.

Toss the cooked pasta with sauce and parsley and serve immediately.

healthy indulgences

Somewhere along the way, comfort food became synonymous with cream, butter, extra cheese and super-sized portions. While I firmly believe that these foods should be enjoyed on occasion, my healthy indulgent recipes prove that comfort food can be light in calories and big on flavor.

For me, the phrase "comfort food" triggers memories of cozy evenings spent in my mother's kitchen, watching her ladle bowls of steaming polenta, simmer homemade red sauce or generously slather butter onto freshly baked bread. As a child, there was no place I would rather be than perched upon a stool, helping my mom and sneaking bites of her latest creation.

Each of these recipes is inspired by the foods I grew up eating, with a nutrient-dense approach. Heavy Alfredo sauce is replaced with a silky, smooth cauliflower cream sauce (page 77), while traditional carbonara sauce gets a plant-based makeover (page 66). While your mind may know the difference, your taste buds will be none the wiser. Get ready to fall in love all over again with healthy comfort food.

LENTIL BOLOGNESE WITH RIGATONI

— SERVES 4–6 —

Is there anything lentils can't do? Cooked lentils are my favorite substitute for ground beef and this sauce is no exception. Praised by both vegetarians and meat eaters, this sauce was a favorite with my recipe testers. While it's ready in under an hour, I prefer to make this on a Sunday afternoon to let it simmer on the stove for hours. The result is a complex, rich, stew-like sauce that goes great over thick rigatoni. Sometimes I forgo the pasta altogether and eat it straight from the bowl with a hunk of crusty bread. Since the sprinkle of Parmesan cheese brings in additional umami flavors, don't skip it. However, it can easily be replaced with a dairy-free version.

LENTIL BOLOGNESE SAUCE

1 cup (200 g) dried brown lentils, rinsed

1 tbsp (15 ml) extra virgin olive oil

1 white onion, chopped

2 celery ribs, chopped

2 medium-sized carrots, chopped

Salt and freshly ground black pepper

3 cloves garlic, minced

1 (28-oz [795-g]) can crushed tomatoes

3 tbsp (55 g) tomato paste

2 tbsp (30 ml) red wine vinegar

1 cup (240 ml) water

1 tsp dried oregano

1 tsp dried rosemary

1 tsp dried thyme

¼ tsp crushed red pepper flakes

¼ cup (25 g) Parmesan cheese, freshly grated, plus more for garnish

⅓ cup (10 g) fresh parsley leaves, chopped

12 oz (340 g) rigatoni pasta (roughly 4½ cups dried pasta)

Place the lentils in a medium stock pan and add water until lentils are covered by at least 2 inches (5 cm). Bring to a boil. Cover, reduce heat to low and simmer until just tender, about 30–35 minutes. Once tender, drain and set aside.

Heat 1 tablespoon (15 ml) olive oil in a large pot over medium heat. Add the onion, celery, carrots and a pinch each of salt and pepper, and cook for 10 minutes or until the onion is translucent and vegetables are soft. Stir in the garlic.

Add the cooked and drained lentils, tomatoes, tomato paste, vinegar, water and dried herbs to the pot, along with the crushed red pepper flakes and a pinch of salt. Stir the mixture well and bring to a boil. Reduce to a simmer and cover. Cook for at least 20 minutes, stirring occasionally, until the sauce has thickened and reduced slightly. This is definitely a Sunday-afternoon sauce, so feel free to let it simmer for longer, just make sure to stir occasionally. Just before serving, stir in the Parmesan cheese and parsley

While the sauce is cooking, bring a large pot of salted water to a boil. Add the rigatoni and cook until al dente. Drain the pasta but do not rinse.

Divide the pasta among 4–6 bowls and top with Bolognese sauce. Top with extra Parmesan cheese, if desired.

VEGAN VERSION: Replace Parmesan cheese with Vegan Parmesan Cheese (page 182), same amount.

RAINBOW PEPPERS WITH CAPELLINI

— SERVES 4–6 —

This is one of my favorite light pastas. The peppers almost melt into the sauce, creating a luxurious dish that tastes much richer than it actually is. While this dish takes a while to come together, actual hands-on time is rather minimal. You can roast the peppers up to two days ahead of time, so plan ahead if you need to.

I kept this one dairy-free for my vegan friends, but feel free to stir in a little Parmesan cheese at the end if desired. Since this is my take on a favorite childhood sandwich—crusty roll, seared sausage and lots of peppers and onions—I sometimes serve this pasta alongside grilled vegetarian sausage. Field Roast makes a vegetarian Italian sausage that tastes great with this peppery pasta.

3 large red bell peppers

3 large yellow bell peppers

1 tbsp (15 ml) extra virgin olive oil

4 large shallots, thinly sliced

Salt, to taste

2 garlic cloves, thinly sliced

⅛ tsp crushed red pepper flakes or more if you like more heat

½ tsp dried oregano

½ tsp dried basil

½ cup (120 ml) vegetable broth

Freshly ground black pepper

10 oz (285 g) capellini (angel hair pasta, a little more than ½ the box)

Preheat the broiler to high and place the rack under the broiler about 4 inches (10 cm) from the heat source. Wash the peppers and place on a foil-lined baking sheet. Broil, turning the peppers as each side starts to blister and brown, until they have collapsed. This should take anywhere from 15–30 minutes depending on the size of your peppers.

Remove the baking sheet from the oven and very carefully slide the peppers into a bowl and cover with a kitchen towel to let steam, about 10 minutes. Remove the towel and let peppers cool until you can handle them, about 15 more minutes. Remove the blistered skins, seeds and stems and thinly slice into strips. It's okay if the peppers fall apart as you do this; you want them finely sliced. This step can be done up to two days ahead of time. If making ahead, place the pepper strips and any juices in a container and refrigerate until ready to use.

While the peppers are broiling, make the sauce. Heat olive oil in a large saucepan over medium heat. Add the shallots and a generous pinch of salt and let cook until the shallots have reduced and are golden brown. Stir in the garlic and add the peppers. Let cook for 5–10 minutes more until the peppers are broken down and shallots are caramelized. Add in the crushed red pepper flakes and herbs and let cook a minute or two more. Add in the vegetable broth, reduce heat to medium-low and let simmer until the sauce has thickened and reduced by ⅓, about 10 minutes. Season to taste with salt and pepper.

Meanwhile, bring a large pot of water to boiling over medium heat. Add the capellini and cook until just under al dente, about 1 minute under the recommended package cooking time. Remove the pasta from the pot and reserve 1 cup (237 ml) of pasta water.

Add the pasta to the saucepan along with ½ cup (118 ml) reserved pasta water. Toss to liberally coat the noodles in the sauce. If it's too dry, add the remainder of the pasta water. Let cook for another minute or two until the pasta is al dente.

TORTELLINI WITH ZUCCHINI AND TEMPEH SAUSAGE

— SERVES 4–6 —

This might be my favorite dish in the entire chapter. I know the idea of tempeh can be off-putting, especially when it's described as a fermented soy bean cake, but in addition to being a great source of protein and fiber, tempeh is easier to digest than most legumes and beans because fermentation aids the process. If you're new to preparing tempeh, start here! Once you taste it sautéed into crumbled "sausage," you may do a double take that you aren't eating actual sausage! Thanks to the abundant use of traditional spices like fennel, crushed red pepper flakes and sage, this tempeh sausage is about as close to the real thing as you can get. Thankfully, it's much lighter and healthier. I make a batch of these crumbles at least weekly. Try them on pizza, in frittatas or tossed in salads.

While the ingredient list seems long, it's mostly various dried spices, many of which are pantry staples.

TEMPEH SAUSAGE

4 oz (115 g) tempeh, crumbled or finely chopped with large knife

1 tsp fennel seed

½ tsp dried basil

½ tsp dried oregano

¼ tsp crushed red pepper flakes

¼ tsp dried sage

1 garlic clove, minced

1 tbsp (15 ml) soy sauce

1 tsp extra virgin olive oil

1 tbsp (15 ml) fresh lemon juice

½ cup (100 g) fresh basil, roughly chopped

⅛ cup (25 g) pine nuts

2 garlic cloves, smashed

Salt and freshly ground black pepper

3 tbsp (45 ml) extra virgin olive oil, divided

9-oz (255-g) package of cheese tortellini

2 medium zucchini, sliced into half-moon shapes

2 tbsp (30 ml) fresh lemon juice

1 tsp lemon zest

Place the tempeh in a sauté pan and cover with water. Bring the water to a boil and let cook, about 10 minutes.

Drain off any remaining water and reduce the heat to medium. Add in the fennel seed, dried basil, oregano, crushed red pepper flakes, sage, garlic clove, soy sauce, olive oil and lemon juice. Cook, stirring occasionally until lightly browned, about 10 minutes. Set aside and wipe out pan.

Place the chopped basil, pine nuts, garlic and a pinch each of salt and pepper into a small food processor or blender. Pulse a few times until combined. With the blade on, slowly pour in 2 tablespoons (30 ml) olive oil until a chunky paste forms. I prefer this to have a little texture to it so I don't finely puree. Set aside.

Bring a pot of salted water to a boil. Add the tortellini and cook until tender. They should float to the top as they finish cooking so you can scoop them up and place them into a separate bowl.

In the wiped-out pan that you used to make the sausage, heat the remaining 1 tablespoon (15 ml) of olive oil over medium heat. Add the zucchini and cook until tender and golden brown. Add the lemon juice to the pan and scrape up any browned bits off the bottom of the pan. Add in the cooked sausage and stir to combine. Add in the cooked tortellini, lemon zest and reserved pesto and toss to combine.

VEGAN VERSION: Carla's Pasta makes a good vegan tortellini with tofu and vegetables. Otherwise, sub in another short pasta like penne or pillowy gnocchi.

PENNE ALLA VODKA

— SERVES 4-6 —

While not a traditional Italian dish, this is one of my favorite Americanized pasta meals. Regardless of where this spicy, vodka-laced tomato sauce originated, it gets regular rotation in my house.

Once again, cashew cream is the star, replacing heavy cream in this plant-based version, swirled into a peppery red sauce. This pink dish is a standout and crowd favorite.

12 oz (340 g) penne pasta

VODKA SAUCE

2 tsp (10 ml) extra virgin olive oil

4 garlic cloves, minced

½ tsp crushed red pepper flakes, or more to taste

1 (28-oz [795-g]) can crushed tomatoes, including juice

¼ cup (60 ml) plain vodka

¼ tsp dried thyme

½ tsp dried oregano

Salt and freshly ground black pepper

½ cup (70 g) raw cashews, soaked for at least 1 hour, then drained

¼ cup (5 g) fresh parsley leaves, finely chopped, plus extra for garnish

Bring a large pot of salted water to a boil. Add the penne to the boiling water and cook until al dente, per package directions. Drain, reserving 1 cup (237 ml) of the pasta water.

Meanwhile, make the sauce. Add the oil to a large saucepan and cook over medium heat. Stir in the garlic and crushed red pepper flakes and cook for 2 minutes, being careful not to burn. Add in the crushed tomatoes with juice, vodka, thyme, oregano and a generous pinch each of salt and pepper. Cook until slightly reduced, about 15 minutes.

Place the soaked and drained cashews, a pinch of salt and ⅓ cup (78 ml) of the pasta water into a high-powered blender and puree until very creamy and smooth. Depending on the power of your blender, this can take up to 5 minutes. If the mixture is too thick, add in more of the pasta water. The overall texture should be similar to heavy cream.

Stir the cashew cream into the cooked pasta and toss to coat the noodles. If the sauce is too thick, thin with reserved pasta water starting with 1–2 tablespoons (15–30 ml) at a time. Stir in the parsley and serve. Garnish with extra chopped parsley, if desired.

PORTOBELLO CARBONARA

— SERVES 4 —

Fettuccine carbonara is one of my favorite pasta dishes. This version uses meaty portobello mushrooms to stand in for traditional pancetta. The chopped mushrooms cook down into crispy, caramelized bits to create a rich, salty taste similar to pancetta.

The trick to this recipe is timing the sauce to be done by the time the pasta is cooked. You need the noodles to be warm enough to melt the raw-egg-and-cheese mixture, ensuring a creamy, silky sauce covering every strand.

1 tbsp (15 ml) extra virgin olive oil

3 shallots, minced

2 garlic cloves, minced

10 oz (285 g) baby portobello mushrooms, chopped

⅛ tsp crushed red pepper flakes, or more to taste

Salt and freshly ground black pepper

8 oz (225 g) whole-wheat fettuccine

1 large egg

½ cup (50 g) Parmesan cheese, freshly grated, plus extra for garnish

Heat a large sauté pan over medium heat and add the olive oil. Add the shallots and cook until soft and caramelized, about 8–10 minutes. Add in the garlic cloves, mushrooms, crushed red pepper flakes and a pinch each of salt and pepper. Cook until soft and golden brown, about 10 more minutes.

Meanwhile, bring a large pot of salted water to a boil. Add the fettucine and cook until al dente, according to package directions. You want the pasta to be hot when you mix the rest of the ingredients in, so time it to finish cooking when the mushrooms are almost ready. Drain and reserve ½ cup (118 ml) of pasta water.

While the pasta is cooking, whisk together the egg, Parmesan cheese and a pinch of pepper.

Turn off the stove and add the hot pasta to the mushroom mixture along with the Parmesan cheese mixture. Stir the ingredients together and add in a little reserved pasta water to thin if needed. Serve with extra Parmesan cheese, if desired.

TOFU PICCATA

— SERVES 4 —

The secret to perfectly prepared tofu is pressing it before cooking. Pressing prevents soggy tofu and allows for a crispy exterior. You can use a fancy tofu press or wrap the tofu in paper towels and place a heavy weight, such as a few food cans, on top. Set aside for at least 15 minutes before slicing. The longer tofu drains, the chewier it will be.

For this piccata recipe, firm tofu is cooked in a delicious sauce of vegan butter, broth, parsley, lemons and capers. The pairing of bright lemon and briny capers is almost magical. When I'm not serving this sauce on crispy tofu, I love it tossed with plain pasta or chickpeas. For a main course, serve this piccata alongside your favorite pasta or roasted fingerling potatoes.

1 lb (455 g) extra firm tofu, sliced into ¼-inch (0.5-cm) thick slices

½ cup (65 g) all-purpose flour

Salt and freshly ground black pepper

2 tbsp (30 ml) plus 1 tbsp (15 ml) extra virgin olive oil, divided

3 tbsp (45 g) unsalted butter, divided

⅓ cup (80 ml) fresh lemon juice

½ cup (120 ml) vegetable broth

¼ cup (70 g) capers

⅛ cup (5 g) fresh parsley leaves, chopped, plus extra for garnish

Drain tofu, wrap in paper towel, and place a heavy object on top for 10–15 minutes to remove any excess water.

Put the flour into a shallow bowl. Season the tofu with small pinch each of salt and pepper and dredge in the flour, tapping off any excess. Place on a plate and set aside.

Heat 2 tablespoons (30 ml) olive oil and 2 tablespoons (30 g) butter in a large skillet over medium-high heat. Add the tofu in batches and cook, turning once, until golden brown on both sides, about 2 minutes. Set aside but do not drain the oil/butter from the skillet.

To the skillet, add the remaining 1 tablespoon (15 g) of butter and 1 tablespoon (15 ml) of olive oil along with the lemon juice, broth and capers. Return to stove and bring to simmer, scraping up brown bits from the skillet for extra flavor. Cook for at least 5 minutes; the sauce will thicken slightly as it cooks. Stir in the parsley.

To serve, place tofu on a platter and pour sauce over to coat. Garnish with parsley, if desired.

VEGAN VERSION: Replace butter with non-dairy butter, same amount.

PUMPKIN FETTUCCINE ALFREDO

— SERVES 6-8 —

Who doesn't love fettuccine alfredo? Cream, butter and cheese: the holy trinity of a delicious, high-calorie meal. Fettuccine alfredo every now and then isn't a big deal. We are all allowed to over-indulge on occasion, but you can make a sauce that is just as creamy and rich, without all the unnecessary cholesterol and saturated fat, and with a fraction of the calories. This vegan version allows fettuccine alfredo to be on the menu a lot more often. A win-win.

The simple addition of pumpkin, sage and nutmeg to cashew cream makes this the perfect fall meal, and fancy enough to serve for others. Serve immediately after making. This sauce will thicken dramatically as it cools, so you want to enjoy it piping hot.

1 lb (455 g) fettuccine pasta (preferably fresh, but dried will work)

PUMPKIN ALFREDO SAUCE

1 cup (200 g) raw cashews, soaked in water for at least 1 hour

2 tbsp (30 ml) fresh lemon juice

1 cup (240 ml) soy or other non-dairy milk

¾ tsp salt, plus more to taste

¼ tsp white pepper, plus more to taste (see note)

1 tsp dried sage

⅛ tsp nutmeg, freshly ground

½ cup (110 g) canned pumpkin

Bring a large pot of salted water to a boil. Add the fettuccine and cook until al dente. Drain, reserving 1 cup (237 ml) of the cooking water.

While the pasta is cooking, make the sauce. In a high-powered blender or food processor, combine the cashews, lemon juice, non-dairy milk, salt and pepper, and blend until very smooth. Depending on the strength of your blender, this could take anywhere from 1–3 minutes.

Add in the dried sage, freshly ground nutmeg and canned pumpkin. Blend for another minute, until combined, then season to taste with more salt and pepper, if needed. Just before serving, toss the sauce with the hot noodles. If sauce is too thick, thin with reserved pasta water.

NOTE: Whenever I make cream sauces like this, I use white pepper instead of black so it doesn't show against the pale-colored sauce. If you already have white pepper in your pantry, use it here. If you don't, no need to rush out and get it. Freshly ground black pepper will work just fine.

CHICKPEA AND MUSHROOM MARSALA

— SERVES 4 —

Who needs chicken when you've got chickpeas? For this hearty dish, I'm swapping in chickpeas and mushrooms for chicken, upping the fiber and protein content of the original dish. After browning the mushrooms and chickpeas in a smidgen of butter, I sprinkle on flour and cook until it's brown and lightly toasted. Then, I add in the flavorful Marsala wine and water and simmer for a thick, luscious sauce to serve over egg noodles.

These days, most well-stocked grocery stores will carry Marsala wine in the alcohol section, but if you can't find it, substitute in ½ cup (118 ml) dry white wine and 2 teaspoons (10 ml) of brandy. The sauce won't have the unique, complex flavor of Marsala wine, but the substitution is fairly close and will work in a pinch.

8 oz (230g) wide egg noodles

2 tbsp (30 g) butter, divided

10 oz (280 g) white, cremini or baby portobello mushrooms, sliced

Salt and freshly ground black pepper

2 cloves garlic, minced

1 cup (165 g) chickpeas, cooked, rinsed and drained if canned

⅛ cup (15 g) flour

⅔ cup (157 ml) Marsala wine, preferably dry

⅓ cup (78 ml) water

1 tsp balsamic vinegar

½ cup (15 g) fresh parsley leaves, chopped

Bring a large pot of salted water to a boil. Add the egg noodles and cook until al dente. Drain and set aside.

Heat 1 tablespoon (15 g) butter in a large skillet over medium heat until melted and starting to sizzle. Add the sliced mushrooms, season with a generous pinch each of salt and pepper and cook, stirring occasionally, until mushrooms are seared and cooked through, about 6–8 minutes. Add the garlic and drained chickpeas and stir to combine. Sprinkle the flour over the mushroom and chickpea mixture, and stir a few times until flour is toasted and no longer white. Take care not to mush the beans and mushrooms together.

Add the Marsala wine and water to the pan, using a wooden spoon or silicone spatula to scrape up any browned butter bits. Reduce the heat to medium low and cook, stirring occasionally, until the sauce thickens, about 5–6 minutes. Remove from heat and stir in the remaining 1 tablespoon (15 g) of butter, balsamic vinegar and parsley. Season with salt and pepper to taste, if necessary, and serve over cooked egg noodles.

VEGAN VERSION: Replace butter with non-dairy butter, same amount. Replace egg noodles with egg-less noodles.

STUFFED PEPPERS

— SERVES 4 —

Stuffed vegetables are an easy way to make a produce-packed dinner take center stage. This is a riff on a favorite recipe from my grandmother. I'm swapping in lentils for the ground beef and adding in a few more vegetables for good measure. When I make these peppers, I usually whip up my Quick Marinara (page 182) while the rice and lentils are cooking. Of course, jarred marinara sauce is also fine. My favorites are Barilla, DeLallo and Trader Joe's Trader Giotto's Tomato and Basil Marinara.

1 cup (190 g) brown rice

1 cup (190 g) brown or green lentils

4 bell peppers, any color

1 tbsp (15 ml) extra virgin olive oil

½ yellow onion, chopped

3 carrots, chopped

2 celery ribs, chopped

½ tsp Italian seasoning

¼ tsp crushed red pepper flakes

Salt and freshly ground black pepper

4 cups (950 ml) marinara sauce

¼ cup (25 g) breadcrumbs

¼ cup (25 g) Parmesan cheese, freshly grated

Place the brown rice and 4 cups (946 ml) water in a medium saucepan and bring to a boil. Reduce heat, add the lentils, cover and simmer for 40–45 minutes until tender. Drain and set aside.

While the rice and lentils are cooking, parboil the peppers. Remove the tops of the peppers and the seeds. Bring a large pot of water to a boil. Add the peppers and cook for 8–12 minutes, depending on the size of your peppers, until just tender. Remove, drain and set aside.

Preheat the oven to 350°F (176°C).

Heat the oil in a large pot or Dutch oven over medium heat. Add the onion, carrots and celery and cook for 8–10 minutes until vegetables are soft and reduced. Stir in Italian seasoning, crushed red pepper flakes and a pinch each of salt and pepper, along with the cooked lentil and rice mixture. Mix in ½ cup (120 ml) of the marinara sauce and season to taste with salt and pepper, if needed.

Place 1 cup (240 ml) of sauce in the bottom of an 8x8-inch (20.5x20.5-cm) or larger glass pan. The peppers can either be stuffed whole or sliced in half and stuffed. Place about 1 cup (185 g) stuffing in each whole pepper cavity, or ½ cup (95 g) in each pepper half. Top each pepper with ½–¾ cup (118–177 ml) of the marinara sauce. Mix together the breadcrumbs and Parmesan cheese and sprinkle over the peppers.

Lightly tent with foil and bake for 30 minutes.

VEGAN VERSION: Replace Parmesan cheese with Vegan Parmesan Cheese (page 182), same amount.

BEET BUTTER LINGUINE

— SERVES 4 —

This unique pasta dish is one of my husband's absolute favorites. The shocking pink color is a fun twist on traditional Italian and features one of my most beloved vegetables, the beet.

Roasted beets are pureed with goat cheese and hazelnuts to create a thick, creamy paste that melts into hot pasta. After cooking the pasta, make sure to reserve the remaining pasta water to add to the linguine and beet puree. The pasta water contains excess starches that help the sauce cling to the noodles, coating every strand. For a beautiful appetizer, try this beet butter puree on toasted crostini.

BEET BUTTER

½ lb (50 g) beets (about 2 medium beets)

3 tsp (15 ml) extra virgin olive oil, divided

8 oz (225 g) linguine

¼ cup (35 g) hazelnuts, toasted and skin removed

3 oz (85 g) goat cheese

1 tbsp (15 ml) balsamic vinegar

3 tbsp (45 ml) vegetable broth

Salt and freshly ground black pepper

3 tbsp (35 g) Parmesan cheese, freshly grated, for garnish

Preheat oven to 400°F (204°C). Wash and scrub beets, removing leaves if attached. Place beets on a large piece of foil and drizzle with 1½ teaspoons (7 ml) of the olive oil. Wrap tightly and place in the oven to roast. Beets are done when they can be easily pierced with a knife, about 50–70 minutes depending on the size of the beets. When done, remove from oven and let cool slightly. Remove skin with a paper towel or by running the beet under cool water and rubbing skin off. This can be done up to three days ahead of time.

Bring a large pot of water to a boil. Add the linguine and cook until al dente, according to package directions. Drain, reserving 1 cup (237 ml) of pasta water.

Quarter beets and place in a food processor with the hazelnuts. Pulse to combine. Add the goat cheese, balsamic vinegar and remaining 1½ teaspoons (7 ml) olive oil. Pulse to combine. Run the food processor and slowly add vegetable broth until the mixture becomes fluffy and smooth. You may not need all the vegetable broth. The beet butter should be smooth and spreadable. Season to taste with salt and pepper.

Place the beet butter in a large bowl (or cooking pot if you don't want to dirty another dish) and add in ⅓ cup (78 ml) of the pasta water. Whisk to thin. Add in the linguine and toss well to combine. If the pasta is too thick, add in more pasta water, 1 tablespoon (15 ml) at a time. Season to taste with salt and pepper. With the creamy goat cheese, I think this dish tastes best with lots of freshly ground black pepper.

Transfer to a serving dish and garnish with Parmesan cheese.

CARAMELIZED ONION FETTUCCINE

— SERVES 4 —

Get ready for your kitchen to smell heavenly! The secret to this pasta is cooking the onions until they're a deep golden brown, intense with flavor to balance the minimal ingredients. They should be mostly broken down, almost melting into the hot pasta to create a simple sauce. To prevent them from becoming mushy, stir only occasionally.

To make this more of a carbonara instead of a cream sauce, omit the cream and beat together one egg with the Parmesan cheese. Add to the hot pasta along with the caramelized onions and serve immediately.

1 tbsp (15 ml) extra virgin olive oil

2 large yellow or white onions, thinly sliced

8 oz (225 g) fettuccine

6 garlic cloves, sliced

1 tsp dried oregano

Salt and freshly ground black pepper

Crushed red pepper flakes, optional, to taste

⅛ cup (30 ml) heavy cream

¼ cup (25 g) Parmesan cheese, freshly grated

Heat the olive oil in a large skillet over medium heat. Add the onions and cook until reduced and dark in color, about 15–20 minutes.

Meanwhile, bring a large pot of salted water to a boil and cook the fettuccine until al dente, according to package directions. Drain, reserving ½ cup (118 ml) pasta water.

Once the onions have caramelized, add the garlic cloves and oregano along with a generous pinch each of salt and pepper. If you like your pasta more on the spicy side, feel free to add in a sprinkle of crushed red pepper flakes. Stir in the heavy cream and add the drained, hot pasta along with ¼ cup (59 ml) reserved pasta water.

Using tongs, quickly toss to combine and add in the Parmesan cheese. If the sauce is too thick, add remaining pasta water to thin.

VEGAN VERSION: Replace heavy cream with Cashew Cream (page 184), same amount. Replace Parmesan cheese with Vegan Parmesan Cheese (page 182), same amount.

CARBONARA WITH TEMPEH BACON

— SERVES 4 —

This one is for those of us who like to incorporate as many healthy foods as possible while still enjoying the rich and satisfying taste of carbonara. I make this tempeh bacon all the time. I can't get enough of the sticky, smoky and slightly sweet tempeh bits. My bet is once you try it, you will love it, too.

Silken tofu is the perfect stand-in for an eggless and cheeseless sauce, thanks to a generous squirt of fresh lemon juice and garlic. Make sure you are getting the silken tofu, as firm won't work the same way. I don't call for it here, as it's an obscure ingredient, but if you've got a little truffle salt or black salt lying around your pantry, add a pinch to the creamy sauce for a hint of that ubiquitous egg flavor.

VEGAN CARBONARA

1 tbsp (15 ml) extra virgin olive oil

1 onion, chopped

4 garlic cloves, chopped

1 (14-oz [395-g]) package soft tofu, drained

⅓ cup (80 ml) vegetable broth

3 tbsp (45 ml) fresh lemon juice

¾ cup (5 g) fresh parsley leaves, chopped, divided

¾ tsp salt

¼ tsp freshly ground black pepper

8 oz (225 g) tempeh

8 oz (225 g) linguine

1 tbsp (30 ml) extra virgin olive oil

3 tbsp (45 ml) soy sauce

2 tbsp (30 ml) maple syrup

2 tbsp (30 ml) balsamic vinegar

½ tsp cumin

¼ tsp crushed red pepper flakes

Freshly ground black pepper, for garnish

Vegan Parmesan Cheese (page 182), for garnish

Heat 1 tablespoon (15 ml) olive oil in a small skillet over medium heat. Add the onion and garlic and cook until soft, about 5–8 minutes. Place cooked onion in a high-powered blender along with the tofu, vegetable broth, lemon juice, ¼ cup (5 g) parsley, salt and pepper. Puree until very soft and creamy. Set aside.

Meanwhile, heat a large pot of water fitted with a steamer basket to boiling. Add the tempeh and steam for 15 minutes. Remove the tempeh and the steamer basket, adding more water if needed. Add the linguine to the pot and cook until al dente, according to package directions. Drain, reserving 1 cup (237 ml) pasta water.

Crumble the steamed tempeh using a box grater or very finely chop. Heat a large skillet over medium heat and add the tempeh along with 1 tablespoon (15 ml) of olive oil, cooking until tempeh is golden brown and slightly crispy, about 5 minutes. Whisk together the soy sauce, maple syrup, balsamic vinegar, cumin and crushed red pepper flakes. Pour mix over the tempeh, reduce heat to medium-low and cook until the liquid is absorbed and tempeh is glazed and crispy, about 10–15 minutes.

To assemble, toss the linguine with the carbonara sauce and add in the tempeh bacon. If the mixture is too thick, thin with some of the reserved pasta water. Stir in ½ cup (15 g) parsley, a generous sprinkle of pepper and vegan Parmesan cheese. Serve immediately.

LINGUINE WITH ARTICHOKE PESTO

— SERVES 4 —

I love this springtime take on pesto, and make it often to spread on grilled tofu or crostini and to use in this pasta. It's a bright, refreshing take on traditional pesto, and comes together in just a few minutes. I served this pesto to my mom a few years ago and she's been raving about it ever since. If it impressed her that much, I know you'll love it too. Canned artichoke hearts are your best bet here as thawed, previously frozen ones tend to hold too much water and lack flavor.

8 oz (225 g) linguine

ARTICHOKE PESTO

1 (8.5-oz [240-g]) can artichoke hearts, drained

1 cup (15 g) fresh basil

½ cup (85 g) almonds

1 large lemon, zested and juiced

2 garlic cloves

⅓ cup (35 g) Parmesan cheese

⅓ cup (80 ml) extra virgin olive oil

¼ cup (60 ml) vegetable broth

Salt and freshly ground black pepper

Parmesan cheese, freshly grated, for garnish

Bring a large pot of salted water to a boil. Add the linguine and cook until al dente, according to package directions. Drain, reserving ½ cup (118 ml) pasta water.

While the pasta is cooking, make the pesto. Place the artichoke hearts, basil, almonds, lemon zest, lemon juice, garlic cloves and Parmesan cheese in the base of a food processor. Pulse a few times to chop together. With the motor running, drizzle in the olive oil and vegetable broth to create a thick paste.

Add the artichoke pesto to the hot linguine and toss to combine. Add a little of the reserved pasta water to thin and season to taste with salt and pepper.

Serve immediately, garnished with extra Parmesan cheese, if desired.

VEGAN VERSION: Replace Parmesan cheese with Vegan Parmesan Cheese (page 182), same amount.

baked pastas

When a day hasn't gone my way or the weather takes a dreary turn, I turn to a comforting bowl of baked pasta for relief. There's nothing like a plate of piping-hot Triple Cheese Baked Vegetable Macaroni (page 72) or Wild Mushroom Lasagna (page 75) to brighten the day and bring a smile to my face.

For company, dishes like Roasted Vegetable Ziti (page 71), Garden Patch Lasagna (page 77) or White Cheddar Mac and Cheese (page 76) are crowd-pleasing hits. Assemble ahead of time and bake once your guests arrive. After your guests enjoy one or two of the options in the antipasti chapter (page 147), they'll be ready to linger around the table enjoying a hearty meal of baked pasta.

ROASTED VEGETABLE ZITI

— SERVES 10–12 —

As fans of my blog know, I prefer roasted vegetables to just about any other preparation out there. It's my secret weapon for making people fall in love with vegetables, as roasting them brings out their naturally sweet flavor. I've made this dish a hundred times yet rarely the same way. The vegetable ingredients below are just a suggestion—feel free to use whatever you have lying around.

This recipe makes a lot, easily serving 10 to 12 adults, so enjoy this when you have friends joining you for dinner or are in the mood for leftovers. Sometimes, I'll make a batch of this and divide it between two baking dishes. One is enjoyed immediately and the other goes into the freezer for a rainy day.

2 cups (250 g) squash (zucchini, summer squash or a mix of both), chopped

2 medium carrots, chopped (about 1 cup [128 g])

2 cups (180 g) broccoli florets, chopped into bite-sized pieces

1 tsp extra virgin olive oil

Salt and freshly ground black pepper

12 oz (340 g) ziti pasta

1 (15-oz [425-g]) container part-skim ricotta cheese

1 large egg, lightly beaten

1¼ cups (140 g) shredded mozzarella cheese, divided

Scant ⅛ tsp nutmeg, freshly ground

¼ tsp crushed red pepper flakes, or to taste

1 (26-oz [737-g]) jar marinara sauce or 3 cups [710 ml] Sunday Red Sauce (page 181)

Preheat oven to 375°F (190°C). Toss the squash, carrots and broccoli with the olive oil and a pinch each of salt and pepper. Mix well and place in a single layer on a baking sheet. (You may need two sheets.) Roast for 35–40 minutes until just tender.

While the vegetables are cooking, make the ziti. Bring a large pot of salted water to a boil and add the ziti. Cook until just al dente, then drain but do not rinse.

In a large bowl, mix together the ricotta cheese, egg, ½ cup (57 g) mozzarella cheese, nutmeg, crushed red pepper flakes and a few cracks of freshly ground pepper. Add the vegetables and pasta to the cheese mixture and stir until just combined.

Reduce oven to 350°F (176°C). Pour 1 cup (237 ml) of the marinara sauce in a 9x13-inch (23x33-cm) baking dish, enough to cover the bottom. Add the ziti mixture and cover with remaining sauce. Top with ¾ cup (85 g) mozzarella. Lightly tent with foil so that the cheese doesn't stick to the foil, and bake for 30 minutes. Remove the foil and cook another 15 minutes until bubbly and hot. Remove from oven and let stand 15 minutes before serving.

NOTE: For easy cleanup, place all of the prepped vegetables in a large mixing bowl. Then, use the same bowl to mix the cooked vegetables in with the pasta and cheese.

TRIPLE CHEESE BAKED VEGETABLE MACARONI

— SERVES 4 —

A baked macaroni for both the kids and the adults! It's comfort food with lots of
colorful vegetables and enough cheese to please everyone.

1 cup (115 g) elbow noodles

2 tbsp (30 g) butter

2 tbsp (15 g) all-purpose flour

1¼ cups (300 ml) low-fat milk

½ cup (45 g) fontina cheese, shredded

Salt and freshly ground black pepper

1½ cups (215 g) zucchini, chopped

½ cup (70 g) frozen peas

½ cup (15 g) fresh basil, finely chopped

½ cup (80 g) ciliegine (mozzarella balls),
cut in half

¼ cup (15 g) panko breadcrumbs

½ cup (30 g) Parmesan cheese, freshly
grated

Bring a medium pot of salted water to a boil. Add the elbow noodles and cook until
al dente according to package directions. Drain and set aside.

Meanwhile, heat the butter in a saucepan over medium heat. Add the flour and
cook to make a golden brown paste, stirring often. Gently whisk in the milk and
cook, stirring, until the milk thickens, about 5 minutes. Stir in the fontina cheese until
melted. Season to taste with a pinch each of salt and pepper.

Preheat the oven to 375°F (190°C).

In a large bowl, toss together the cooked noodles, cheese sauce, zucchini and peas.
Stir until noodles and vegetables are coated. Stir in the basil and mozzarella. Place in
an 8x8-inch (20.5x20.5-cm) baking dish.

Mix together the breadcrumbs and Parmesan cheese and sprinkle over the top of
the noodles. Bake for 20 minutes until hot and bubbly. Remove from oven and let sit
for 5 minutes before serving.

WILD MUSHROOM LASAGNA

— SERVES 8–12 —

There are quite a few steps here, but there's nothing better than homemade lasagna on a chilly winter night. Creamy béchamel and a reduction of woodsy, earthy, wild mushrooms take this lasagna to another level. Everyone I make this for raves about the unique, complex flavor. To cut down on the fat and calories, I'm using a cauliflower cream sauce in place of traditional béchamel. For the marinara, I advocate using a homemade sauce since you are already putting in so much work, but any jarred sauce will work for faster prep.

CAULIFLOWER BÉCHAMEL

5 cups (540 g) cauliflower florets (one head of cauliflower)

4 tbsp (55 g) butter

¼ cup (45 g) all-purpose flour

4 cups (950 ml) skim or low-fat milk

⅛ tsp nutmeg, freshly ground

¼ cup (30 g) Parmesan cheese, freshly grated

Salt and freshly ground black pepper

1 lb (455 g) low-fat ricotta cheese

1 large egg

¾ cup (20 g) fresh parsley leaves, chopped, divided

½ tsp dried thyme

¼ cup (30 g) Parmesan cheese, freshly grated

Salt and freshly ground black pepper

1 tbsp (15 ml) extra virgin olive oil

3 garlic cloves, minced

3 shallots, finely diced

1 lb (445 g) mixed mushrooms or mushrooms of choice, chopped

¼ cup (60 ml) white wine or vegetable broth

3 cups (700 ml) marinara sauce

16 lasagna noodles, no-boil or cooked

¾ cup (80 g) fontina cheese, freshly grated

Place cauliflower florets in a large microwave-safe bowl with enough water to just cover the bottom of the bowl. Cover bowl loosely with a paper towel and steam cauliflower in microwave on high until tender, 4–5 minutes; drain. Alternatively, you can bring a pot of water to a boil and place cauliflower in a steam basket and cook until fork tender, about 4–5 minutes; drain.

Melt the butter in a saucepan over medium heat. Whisk in the flour and cook for one minute until golden brown. Gently whisk in the milk and increase the heat to medium high and bring to a boil. Continue to whisk, cooking until thick, about 5 minutes. Add in the cauliflower, reduce heat to low and simmer for another 5 minutes.

Remove from heat and let cool slightly. Transfer to a high-powered blender or food processor and puree until very smooth. Alternatively, use an immersion blender to puree. Add in the nutmeg, Parmesan cheese and a pinch each of salt and pepper, and pulse a few times to combine. It should be the consistency of marinara sauce. If it's too thick, thin with more milk.

Combine the ricotta, egg, ½ cup (20 g) parsley, thyme and Parmesan in a bowl and mix until combined. Season with a pinch each of salt and pepper and set aside.

Heat olive oil in a large sauté pan over medium-high heat. Add in the garlic and shallots and cook for a minute or two until just soft. Add in the mushrooms and cook until tender and golden brown, about 10 minutes. Add the white wine or broth to the pan to deglaze and scrape up any browned bits. Cook until the liquid is completely reduced, about 5 more minutes. Stir in the remaining ¼ cup (10 g) of parsley and season to taste with salt and pepper. Set aside. Preheat oven to 375°F (190°C).

Assemble the lasagna: Ladle a scoop of the tomato sauce into a large baking dish (preferably 11x15-inch [28x38-cm]) to form a thin layer and add a scoop of the cauliflower cream sauce on top. Top with 4 noodles and gently spread ⅓ of the ricotta mixture on top. Evenly spread on ⅓ of the mushroom mixture, then a scoop each of tomato sauce and cauliflower cream sauce. Repeat to make two more layers in this order: noodles, ricotta mixture, mushroom mixture, tomato sauce and cauliflower cream sauce. End with a layer of noodles, cauliflower cream sauce and marinara sauce. Sprinkle with grated fontina cheese.

Place lasagna on a large baking sheet, tent with aluminum foil and bake for 30 minutes. Uncover and bake until bubbly, 20 more minutes. Remove from oven and let sit for 15 minutes before slicing and serving.

WHITE CHEDDAR MAC AND CHEESE

— SERVES 4 —

Both my husband and two-year-old niece can't get enough of this dish, a faux mac and cheese made from a cauliflower cream sauce and lots of grated white cheddar cheese. Using cauliflower as a base instead of a heavy roux cuts down on both fat and calories, but you wouldn't know it once you taste it. The cauliflower sauce blends into the background, allowing the sharp cheddar to shine through. When I'm in a hurry I skip the baked part, but I think it's much better under a crispy crust of breadcrumbs and more cheese.

3 cups (300 g) cauliflower florets

8 oz (225 g) mini shells, mini penne pasta, pasta wheels or other small pasta shape

1 tbsp (15 g) butter

2 large cloves garlic, minced

¼ tsp salt

¼ tsp freshly ground black pepper

½ cup (120 ml) low-fat milk

½ cup (120 ml) water

1½ cups (170 g) white cheddar cheese, shredded

¼ cup (25 g) breadcrumbs

⅛ cup (15 g) Parmesan cheese, freshly and finely grated

1 tsp dried parsley

Place cauliflower and 3 cups (710 ml) of water into a medium saucepan and bring to a boil. Reduce heat to medium low, cover and steam for 10–15 minutes until cauliflower is very soft. Remove from heat, drain and set aside.

While the cauliflower is cooking, bring a large pot of salted water to a boil and add the pasta. Cook until al dente according to package directions. Drain and set aside. In the empty pot you cooked the pasta in, add the butter over medium heat, then add the garlic. Cook until garlic is soft but not burnt, about 2–3 minutes.

Preheat the oven to 350°F (176°C). Place the cooked garlic, steamed cauliflower, salt, pepper, milk and ½ cup (118 ml) water into a high-powered blender and puree until creamy and smooth. Depending on the power of your blender, you may need to add more water.

Return the cauliflower sauce back to the saucepan over medium heat. Whisk in the shredded cheese and stir until melted. Season to taste with salt and pepper and stir in the cooked noodles.

Pour the macaroni mixture to a lightly greased 8x8-inch (20.5x20.5-cm) baking dish. Mix together the breadcrumbs, Parmesan cheese and parsley and sprinkle over the cooked macaroni. Bake for 30 minutes until top is golden brown and mixture is bubbly.

GARDEN PATCH LASAGNA

— SERVES 8–12 —

This recipe proves that even lasagna can get a nutrient-dense makeover. Even though this dish tastes like Alfredo lasagna, it's incredibly light thanks to a creamy, cauliflower-based sauce and more than three pounds (1.3 kg) of fresh vegetables.

CAULIFLOWER SAUCE

1 tbsp (15 ml) extra virgin olive oil, plus more or olive oil spray to coat baking dish

1½ lb (680 g) zucchini and/or yellow squash, thinly sliced

1 lb (455 g) eggplant, chopped

1 large red bell pepper, cut in strips

8 oz (225 g) white button mushrooms, sliced

4 large cloves garlic, minced

2 tsp (2 g) dried oregano

1 tsp dried basil

Salt and freshly ground black pepper

5 cups (500 g) cauliflower florets

1 tbsp (15 g) butter

5 large cloves garlic, minced

1 tsp salt plus more to taste

½ tsp freshly ground black pepper plus more to taste

¾ cup (180 ml) low-fat milk

½ cup (118 ml) water

½ cup (50 g) Parmesan cheese, freshly grated

16 lasagna noodles or whole-wheat noodles, cooked al dente according to package directions, drained and cooled; or no-cook noodles

8 oz (55 g) shredded mozzarella

Heat a large Dutch oven over medium heat and add olive oil. Add in the zucchini, eggplant, red bell pepper, mushrooms, garlic, oregano and basil and cook for 20–25 minutes until vegetables are reduced, cooked through and slightly caramelized. Season to taste with a pinch each of salt and pepper.

While the vegetables are cooking, steam the cauliflower. Add the cauliflower florets and 6 cups (1.4 L) water to a saucepan and bring to a boil. Reduce heat to medium low, cover and steam for 10 minutes until cauliflower is very soft. Remove from heat, drain and set aside.

While the cauliflower is cooking, heat the butter in a small saucepan over medium heat and add the garlic. Cook until garlic is soft but not burnt, about 2–3 minutes. When cauliflower and garlic are done, put them plus 1 teaspoon salt, ¼ teaspoon pepper, the milk and water into a high-powered blender and puree until creamy and smooth. Depending on the power of your blender, you may need to add more water. It should be the consistency of marinara sauce. Stir in the Parmesan cheese.

Preheat oven to 375°F (191°C). To assemble, lightly grease a 9x13-inch (23x33-cm) baking dish with olive oil or olive oil spray. Spread about 1 cup (237 ml) of the cauliflower sauce on the bottom of the dish, enough to cover in a single layer. Top with a layer of noodles. Then layer with ⅓ of the vegetable mixture and ½ cup (55 g) of the shredded cheese and ½ cup (118 ml) of the cauliflower sauce. Repeat two times to make 3 layers in all. End with a layer of noodles, the remaining sauce and ½ cup (55 g) shredded cheese.

Bake for 30–35 minutes or until top is golden brown and bubbly. Remove from oven and let set for 10 minutes before cutting and serving.

CHEESY LASAGNA FOR FOUR

— SERVES 4 —

This is a weeknight lasagna for the times you don't want to be eating lasagna for days on end afterwards—a perfect fit for two to four, with lunch leftovers. Similar in flavor to a red-sauce vegetable lasagna, it's a good choice when you want the comfort of lasagna without the hours in the kitchen. Since I make this on the weeknights, I rely on jarred sauce and no-boil noodles as shortcuts.

1 tbsp (15 ml) extra virgin olive oil

2-3 cloves garlic, minced

6 cups (180 g) fresh spinach, roughly chopped

1 cup (250 g) part-skim ricotta cheese

1 large egg

½ tsp dried oregano

1 tsp dried parsley

Nutmeg, freshly ground

Salt and freshly ground black pepper

¼ cup (25 g) Parmesan cheese, freshly grated

4 cups (946 ml [about 1 jar]) marinara

10 no-boil or oven-ready lasagna noodles

12 thin slices mozzarella cheese

Heat the olive oil and garlic over medium heat in a large skillet. Sauté until soft, about 1 minute, and add the spinach. Cook until just wilted, another minute or two.

Mix together the ricotta cheese, egg, oregano, parsley, a pinch each of nutmeg, salt and pepper in a medium bowl. Stir in the Parmesan cheese.

Preheat the oven to 375°F (190°C). Place about 1 cup (237 ml) of the sauce in the bottom of an 8x8-inch (20.5x20.5-cm) glass baking dish, just enough to cover. Add a layer of noodles (you may have to tuck/cut to fit), ⅓ of the ricotta mixture, ⅓ of the spinach, 4 slices of mozzarella cheese and ½ cup (118 ml) marinara sauce. Repeat to make another two layers, ending with noodles, sauce and 4 slices of cheese.

Bake for 30 minutes until bubbly and hot. Remove from oven and let sit 10 minutes before cutting and serving.

MANICOTTI WITH LENTIL RAGÙ

— SERVES 6–8 —

Hearty and healthy, this protein-packed ragù will keep you satisfied for hours. Lentils are my favorite swap for ground beef, and they taste incredible in this rich vegetable sauce. While it's great on any pasta, I love it served with stuffed manicotti for an impressive, date-night-in meal.

1 cup (190 g) green or brown lentils

1 lb (455 g) manicotti shells

1 tbsp (15 ml) olive oil

½ cup (60 g) onion, chopped

3 garlic cloves, minced

4 oz (115 g) mushrooms (about ½ cup), chopped

1 cup (100 g) celery, chopped

1 cup (110 g) carrots, chopped

¼ tsp crushed red pepper flakes

Salt

4 cups (960 ml) tomato sauce (I prefer Hunt's or Muir Glen)

Freshly ground black pepper

⅛ cup (5 g) fresh basil, chopped

¼ cup (5 g) fresh parsley leaves, chopped

24 oz (680 g) ricotta cheese

¼ cup (5 g) fresh parsley leaves, chopped

½ tsp dried oregano

Salt and freshly ground black pepper

Place the lentils and water in a medium saucepan and bring to a boil. Reduce heat to medium low, cover and cook until lentils are tender, about 35 minutes.

Meanwhile, bring a separate large pot of water to a boil. Add the manicotti shells and cook until just al dente. Drain and set aside.

While the lentils and pasta are cooking, prep the vegetables and make the sauce. Place olive oil in the bottom of a medium saucepan or Dutch oven over medium heat. Add the onion and garlic and cook until onions are translucent, about 5–8 minutes. Add in the mushrooms, celery, carrots, crushed red pepper flakes and a pinch of salt, and cook an additional 10 minutes, stirring often, until vegetables are tender. Add in the tomato sauce and cooked lentils. Reduce heat to low and simmer for 15 minutes, stirring often. Season to taste with salt and pepper, then add in the basil and parsley leaves.

Stir together the ricotta, parsley, oregano and a pinch each of salt and pepper in a separate bowl.

Assemble the manicotti. Preheat the oven to 350°F (176°C).

Place 2 cups (473 ml) of lentil ragu in the bottom of a 9x13-inch (23x33-cm) baking pan. Add the ricotta mixture into each of the manicotti noodles, about ⅓ cup (40 g) per noodle.

For ease, put the ricotta mixture into a pastry bag or plastic bag with the corner snipped off. From there, you can easily pipe the ricotta mixture into the cooked noodles. If you prefer not to, gently spoon the ricotta mixture into the cooked noodles, taking care not to tear the noodles.

Place the filled noodles into a baking dish and cover with the remaining sauce. Cover with foil and bake for 35 minutes.

Remove from the oven and let sit for 5 minutes before serving.

VEGAN OPTION: Sub Vegan Tofu Ricotta (page 187).

EGGPLANT ROLLATINI

— SERVES 4 (12–16 EGGPLANT SLICES) —

It's eggplant Parmesan with a twist—literally. Instead of fried cutlets, strips of eggplant are grilled until meaty and tender, then rolled up with an herb-ricotta mixture and baked in marinara sauce. I think these taste best with my Sunday Red Sauce (page 181).

1 tbsp (15 ml) extra virgin olive oil

2 medium eggplants, sliced ¼-inch (0.5-cm) thick

8 oz (225 g) part-skim ricotta

1 large egg, beaten

¼ cup (5 g) fresh parsley leaves, finely chopped

¼ tsp crushed red pepper flakes

Cinnamon or nutmeg, freshly ground

Salt and freshly ground black pepper

4 cups (960 ml) marinara sauce

Preheat oven to 350°F (176°C).

Heat the olive oil in a grill pan over medium heat. Add the eggplant slices in batches, grilling for 2–3 minutes per side until soft and tender. Set aside.

Mix together the ricotta, egg, parsley, crushed red pepper flakes, a very small pinch of cinnamon or nutmeg, and a pinch each of salt and pepper.

Place 1½ cups (355 ml) of the marinara sauce in the bottom of an 8x8-inch (20.5x20.5-cm) square baking pan. Spread about 2 tablespoons (15 g) of the ricotta mixture onto the grilled eggplant slices and roll up tightly. Place seam down into the marinara sauce and continue with remaining eggplant.

Cover with remaining marinara sauce and cook for 30 minutes until bubbly. Remove, let sit for 5 minutes and serve.

VEGAN OPTION: Sub Vegan Tofu Ricotta (page 187) for ricotta, same amount.

MINI EGGPLANT TIMBALES

— SERVES 4 —

Timbales are portion-perfect ramekins of pasta stuffed inside a grilled eggplant shell. If you like baked pasta and eggplant, you must try this recipe. One part lasagna, one part ziti, these eggplant purses are a fun meal, great to try when eggplant is in peak season. Enjoy as a main meal or as a side dish for protein with a large, bounty-filled salad.

Cooking spray or extra virgin olive oil for the grill pan

1 large eggplant (about 1.2 lb [545 g]), peeled and sliced lengthwise into ¼-inch (0.5-cm) thick slabs

2 cups (230 g) mini penne pasta or other mini pasta

1 cup (250 g) low-fat ricotta cheese

¼ cup (30 g) shredded mozzarella cheese

⅛ tsp crushed red pepper flakes

¼ cup (5 g) fresh basil, chopped, plus more to garnish

Salt and freshly ground black pepper

2 cups (475 ml) marinara sauce

Parmesan cheese, freshly grated, to garnish

Preheat the oven to 375°F (190°C).

Lightly grease the inside of 4 small ramekins. Lightly spray or rub a bit of olive oil on a grill pan so the eggplant doesn't stick. Place the grill pan on the stove over medium heat and add the eggplant slices. Grill until eggplant is tender and soft, about 3–5 minutes per size. You may need to do this in batches, depending on how large your grill pan is. The eggplant slices should be able to fold inside the ramekins so if the slices are too thick, slice them in half lengthwise.

Bring a pot of salted water to a boil and add the penne. Cook until al dente according to package directions. Drain and place in a medium bowl. Add the ricotta, mozzarella, crushed red pepper flakes, basil and pinch each of salt and pepper. Mix together.

Lay the eggplant in the ramekins so there is an overhang. I place one into the ramekin so that there is overhang over the side and continue in a clockwise pattern. Fill the eggplant ramekin with cooked pasta and then gently fold the overhanging eggplant over the filling to enclose. Continue to fill the remaining ramekins and lightly cover with foil. Place in the oven and cook for 20 minutes.

The last 10 minutes of cooking, heat the marinara sauce. Remove the timbales from oven and place ¼ cup (59 ml) of marinara sauce on a plate. Invert the timbales onto the marinara sauce and top with another ¼ cup (59 ml) of marinara. Garnish with Parmesan cheese and basil.

STUFFED SHELLS WITH PEAS AND ASPARAGUS IN PESTO CREAM SAUCE

— SERVES 4–5 (MAKES 20 JUMBO SHELLS) —

Though they are a little more labor intensive than homemade lasagna, stuffed shells are quite possibly my favorite baked pasta dish. For this recipe, I wanted to incorporate as many vegetables as possible while still keeping the creamy, indulgent taste. Ricotta cheese is mixed with asparagus, peppers and peas, then tucked into shells and topped with a cauliflower-pesto cream sauce. It's my lightened-up version of baked Alfredo shells. The bright green and red colors poking out from the cheesy shells are fun for kids and a reminder that most dishes improve with a vegetable makeover.

12 oz (340 g) jumbo shells (roughly 20 shells)

PESTO CREAM SAUCE

4 cups (920 g) cauliflower florets

1 tsp extra virgin olive oil

2 tbsp (20 g) fresh garlic, minced

¾ tsp salt

½ tsp freshly ground black pepper

½ cup (118 ml) low-fat milk

½–¾ cup (118–177 ml) water

½ cup (125 g) prepared pesto

1 tbsp (15 ml) extra virgin olive oil

1 shallot, minced

1 cup (150 g) spring peas

1½ cups (190 g) asparagus, chopped

½ large red bell pepper, chopped

1½ cups (360 g) ricotta cheese

Nutmeg, freshly ground

Salt and freshly ground black pepper

½ cup (55 g) shredded mozzarella

¼ cup (45 g) Parmesan cheese, freshly grated

Bring a large pot of salted water to a boil. Add the shells and cook until just al dente according to package directions. Drain and set aside.

While the pasta is cooking, steam the cauliflower. Add the cauliflower florets and 4 cups (950 ml) water to a saucepan and bring to a boil. Reduce heat to medium low, cover and steam for 10–15 minutes until cauliflower is very soft. Alternatively, you can steam the cauliflower in the microwave. Remove from heat, drain and set aside.

While the cauliflower is cooking, heat olive oil in a small saucepan over medium heat and add the garlic. Cook until garlic is soft but not burnt, about 2–3 minutes. Add the garlic, steamed cauliflower, salt, pepper, milk and ½ cup (118 ml) water into a high-powered blender and puree until creamy and smooth. Depending on the power of your blender, you may need to add more water. Once sauce is creamy and smooth, stir in the pesto. Set aside.

Heat 1 tablespoon (15 ml) olive oil and shallot in a large skillet over medium heat. Add in the peas, asparagus and red bell pepper and cook until vegetables are tender, about 5–7 minutes. Remove from heat and let come to room temperature. Place in a medium bowl along with the ricotta cheese, nutmeg, a pinch each of salt and pepper and shredded mozzarella.

Preheat the oven to 350°F (176°C).

Place ½ of the Pesto Cream Sauce in the bottom of a 9x13-inch (23x33-cm) pan. Stuff the shells with the vegetable filling and place in the Pesto Cream Sauce. Toss with remaining Pesto Cream Sauce to cover and sprinkle with grated Parmesan cheese.

Bake for 35 minutes, until top is golden brown and the sauce is bubbly.

SPINACH LASAGNA ROLLS

— SERVES 4 —

I just love how cute and colorful these lasagna rolls look! I jokingly refer to this dish as my portion-controlled lasagna. Individual noodles are covered with vegetables and ricotta, and then rolled up into single servings.

12 oz (340 g) part-skim ricotta cheese

¾ cup (85 g) shredded mozzarella

Nutmeg, freshly ground

Salt and freshly ground pepper

1 tsp olive oil

2 cloves garlic, minced

6 oz (170 g) fresh baby spinach leaves (about 6 cups)

2 cups (480 ml) marinara sauce

10 cooked (600 g) lasagna noodles (no-boil noodles will not work)

Place the ricotta, mozzarella, and a pinch each of nutmeg, salt and pepper in a medium bowl and set aside.

Heat the olive oil over medium heat in a large skillet and add in the garlic and spinach. Cook, stirring often, until spinach is wilted. Drain off any excess liquid and finely chop the cooked spinach. Add the chopped spinach to the ricotta and season to taste, if needed, with salt and pepper.

Preheat oven to 350°F (176°C). Place 1 cup (237 ml) of the marinara sauce in the bottom of an 8x8-inch (20.5x20.5-cm) glass baking dish. Place 1 cooked lasagna noodle on a cutting board and spread with about ¼ cup (30 g) filling. Gently roll up, tucking the noodle underneath as you go. Place seam-side down in the sauce and continue with remaining noodles. Cover with the remaining marinara sauce and bake for 25–30 minutes.

Remove from oven and serve.

real italians eat grains

When we think of Italian food, most of us instantly think of pasta, and for good reason. However, there are plenty of grains used in Italian cuisine that are just as good—if not better—than pasta. Farro, arborio rice and polenta star in these recipes. Take advantage of the wonderful grains out there and enjoy exploring fresh takes on classic recipes. Many grocery stores are expanding their international sections and carry these grains, but if you have any difficulty finding them, consider ordering them online or drop by an Italian or international market in your city.

WILD MUSHROOM RAGÙ WITH CREAMY POLENTA

— SERVES 4–6 —

This is what healthy comfort food is supposed to taste like. This stick-to-your-ribs meal is creamy, decadent and rich, never mind that it's both vegan and gluten free. A few of my recipe testers said this was their favorite recipe in the entire book, confirming my suspicions that everyone loves creamy polenta topped with an earthy, lush sauce. While wild mushrooms are preferred here, they can be a splurge, so feel free to substitute white button or cremini mushrooms as needed.

WILD MUSHROOM RAGÙ

⅓ cup (80 ml) extra virgin olive oil

4 cups (280 g) mixed wild mushrooms, chopped

Salt and freshly ground black pepper

2 cloves garlic, minced

1 shallot, minced

1 tsp dried rosemary

1 tsp dried oregano

½ cup (120 ml) tomato sauce

¼ cup (60 ml) red wine

CREAMY POLENTA

1 cup (240 ml) vegetable broth

3 cups (709 ml) soy milk

1 cup (170 g) cornmeal

3 tbsp (40 g) non-dairy butter

Salt and freshly ground black pepper

½ cup (120 ml) vegetable broth

1 tbsp (15 g) non-dairy butter

⅛ cup (15 g) fresh parsley leaves, chopped

Heat the olive oil in a large saucepan or Dutch oven over medium heat. Add mushrooms and cook for 10 minutes until reduced and caramelized, stirring only a few times. Season with salt and pepper to taste. Add garlic, shallot, rosemary and oregano, and cook for 5 more minutes. Add tomato sauce and red wine, stir and cook an additional 5 minutes while you prepare the polenta.

In a separate saucepan, heat the broth and milk over medium heat. When bubbles start to surface, gently whisk in cornmeal and stir together. Reduce heat to low and let cook until thick, stirring often, about 15 to 20 minutes. Stir in non-dairy butter and a pinch each of salt and pepper.

While the polenta is simmering, finish the ragù. Add the vegetable broth to the mushroom sauce, reduce heat to low and simmer until polenta is done cooking. Remove the ragù from heat and whisk in 1 tablespoon (15 g) butter. Garnish with parsley.

QUINOA CAPRESE SALAD

— SERVES 4 AS A SIDE DISH, 2 AS A MAIN —

I'm fairly certain I created this recipe as a way to eat caprese salad almost every day and not feel bad about it. Juicy tomatoes, creamy mozzarella and aromatic basil top my list of favorite foods. Adding a base of quinoa makes this a lunch-friendly option with plenty of fiber and protein. For a special treat, I'm calling for burrata cheese, a creamy, milky mozzarella that almost melts into the quinoa and balsamic dressing. If you can't find burrata, substitute fresh buffalo mozzarella instead.

½ cup (85 g) white quinoa, rinsed

1 cup (240 ml) water

Salt

1 garlic clove

DRESSING

2 tbsp (30 ml) fresh lemon juice

1 tbsp (15 ml) balsamic vinegar, plus extra for drizzling

2 tbsp (30 ml) extra virgin olive oil

Freshly ground black pepper

2 large tomatoes, sliced

½ cup (5 g) fresh basil, torn

4 oz (113 g) burrata cheese, sliced

Place the quinoa, water and a pinch of salt in a medium saucepan and bring to a boil. Cover, reduce heat to low and simmer for 10–12 minutes until water is absorbed. Remove from heat and let stand without touching for 5 minutes. Remove lid and gently fluff with a fork.

Finely mince the garlic clove using a sharp knife, then gently run the flat side of the blade on top of the garlic to create a paste. Add the paste to a small mixing bowl and whisk in the lemon juice, balsamic vinegar and olive oil. Add in a pinch each of salt and pepper.

Add the dressing to the quinoa and toss to combine.

Divide the quinoa among 4 bowls and garnish with tomatoes, basil and burrata cheese. Drizzle with balsamic vinegar and enjoy immediately.

FARROTTO PRIMAVERA

— SERVES 6 —

If you can cook risotto, you can cook farrotto. Essentially, this recipe uses farro in place of rice and cooks it in the same manner as you would making a traditional risotto dish. A bolder, more robust grain than arborio rice, farro is chewy, meaty and fantastic paired with spring vegetables.

You can find farro in perlato (pearled), semi-perlato (semi-pearled) and whole varieties. While whole and semi-pearled will contain more fiber and nutrient-rich bran, it can be challenging to find them at regular markets. Since it's more readily available, I call for the pearled variety here, which still packs a whopping five grams of fiber and seven grams of protein per one-fourth-cup serving. If you can get your hands on the less-processed versions, you'll need to add more broth and increase the cooking time to ensure a tender grain.

2 tsp (10 ml) extra virgin olive oil

1 cup (115 g) onion, chopped

5 cups (1.2 L) vegetable broth

3 garlic cloves, minced

1 cup (165 g) pearled (perlato) farro

½ cup (120 ml) white wine

1 cup (105 g) fresh or frozen green peas, thawed

2 cups (280 g [about 1 bunch]) asparagus, chopped

1 cup (80 g) frozen spinach leaves, thawed and excess water squeezed out, or 2 cups (160 g) fresh

¼ tsp crushed red pepper flakes

½ cup (15 g) fresh parsley, chopped

⅓ cup (35 g) Parmesan cheese, freshly grated

1 tbsp (15 g) butter

Salt and freshly ground black pepper

Heat the olive oil over medium heat in a large saucepan. Add in the onion and cook until translucent, about 6–8 minutes. While the onion is cooking, place the broth in a medium saucepan over medium-low heat.

Add the garlic and farro to the onion skillet and cook until the farro is just toasted. Add the white wine and cook until liquid is almost completely absorbed.

Add in the vegetable broth, a ladle at a time (about ¼–½ cup [59–118 ml]), to the farro and stir until liquid is absorbed. Continue to slowly add in the vegetable broth, stirring until completely absorbed, about 25–30 minutes. You may not need all of the broth.

When the farro is almost done yet still chewy, add in the peas, asparagus, spinach and crushed red pepper flakes. Once the farro is creamy and cooked through, stir in the parsley, Parmesan cheese and butter. Season to taste with salt and pepper. Depending on the saltiness of your vegetable broth, you may not need any additional salt.

VEGAN VERSION: Replace Parmesan cheese with Vegan Parmesan Cheese (page 182), same amount. Replace butter with non-dairy butter, same amount.

GOAT CHEESE POLENTA
WITH BLISTERED TOMATOES

— SERVES 4 —

When I dream of comfort food, I dream of this polenta bowl topped with blistered tomatoes and goat cheese. It's creamy, cozy and perfect for the transition from summer to the crisp evenings of fall.

Even though tomatoes are one of my favorite foods, I try hard to enjoy them only when they are at their peak: A juicy July tomato is not the same as a December tomato. To enjoy the bright flavor of tomatoes year round, I favor cherry tomatoes cooked like this—simmered in a saucepan with olive oil and garlic until they burst, creating a blistered tomato skin and plenty of sweet, aromatic sauce. While these tomatoes pair perfectly with goat cheese polenta, the blistered tomatoes also go great on top of crostini, scrambled eggs or hot pasta.

3 cups (709 ml) vegetable broth

1 cup (236 ml) milk

1 cup (145 g) cornmeal

½ tsp salt plus more to taste

Freshly ground black pepper

4 oz (110 g) goat cheese

1 tbsp (15 ml) extra virgin olive oil

5 cups (455 g) cherry tomatoes

2 garlic cloves, finely chopped

1 tbsp (15 ml) red wine vinegar

½ cup (10 g) fresh basil, chopped

Heat vegetable broth and milk in a medium saucepan over medium heat. When bubbles start to surface, gently whisk in the cornmeal and stir together. Reduce heat to low and cook until thick, stirring often, about 15–20 minutes. Season with salt and pepper to taste. Gently stir in the goat cheese and whisk until melted and smooth.

While the polenta is cooking, make the tomatoes. Heat a large skillet over medium-high heat and add the olive oil. When the oil starts to shimmer, add the tomatoes and the garlic and shake gently to distribute tomatoes in a single layer in the skillet. Cook for 10-15 minutes until tomatoes burst and start to form a sauce. Stir the tomatoes often so that they don't stick to the bottom of the skillet and the garlic doesn't burn. Once finished, add in the red wine vinegar and stir in basil. Season with a pinch each of salt and pepper.

Divide polenta among 4 bowls and top with blistered tomatoes.

SPRING VEGETABLE RISOTTO WITH PEA COULIS

— SERVES 6 —

Dining in Napa Valley is an experience like nothing else. Every restaurant, even the small mom-and-pop sandwich shops, features local, gourmet food paired with incredible wine. It's a vacation for your senses, a place we escaped to often when we were living in Northern California. After a full day of wine tasting, we'd often retire to Hurley's, a Yountville restaurant famous for California-inspired cuisine. This is my attempt at one of my favorite Hurley's dishes, a Spring Vegetable Risotto with Pea Coulis and pea shoot salad. The layering of hearty vegetable risotto, minty pea coulis and pea shoot salad is a welcome sign that spring produce has finally arrived. It's dramatic, fresh and a must make.

SPRING VEGETABLE RISOTTO

2 tbsp (30 ml) extra virgin olive oil, divided

2 medium leeks, cleaned and thinly sliced

Salt and freshly ground black pepper

2 cloves garlic, minced

½ cup (55 g) carrots, diced

1 red bell pepper, chopped

2 small yellow squashes, chopped

4 cups (960 ml) vegetable broth

¼ tsp crushed red pepper flakes

⅛ tsp cayenne pepper

⅛ tsp sweet paprika

1 cup (185 g) arborio rice

1 bunch asparagus, chopped

1 cup (180 g) cherry tomatoes, quartered

1 cup (160 g) spring peas, shelled or thawed

2 tbsp (10 g) nutritional yeast

PEA COULIS

2 cups (320 g) peas, fresh or thawed

2 cloves garlic

1 tsp dried mint or 1 tbsp (2.5 g) fresh mint, chopped

¼ cup (5 g) fresh basil

2 tbsp (30 ml) extra virgin olive oil

2 tsp (30 ml) white wine vinegar

PEA SHOOT SALAD

½ cup (35 g) pea shoots, torn

½ tsp extra virgin olive oil

¼ tsp white balsamic vinegar

Salt and freshly ground black pepper

In a Dutch oven or large stockpot, heat 1 tablespoon (15 ml) olive oil over medium heat. Add the leeks, a pinch each of salt and pepper, and cook 10 minutes until soft. Add in the garlic, carrots, red bell pepper and squash. Stir often, cooking until vegetables are tender, about 10 more minutes.

Meanwhile, heat the vegetable broth in a separate pot.

To the vegetable stockpot, add the crushed red pepper flakes, cayenne pepper, paprika and a pinch each of salt and pepper. Cook for another 2–3 minutes. Once vegetables are soft, remove from pot.

SPRING VEGETABLE RISOTTO WITH PEA COULIS

If the bottom of the empty stockpot is dry, add 1 tablespoon (15 ml) olive oil. If there is still liquid left, you don't need to add the oil. Add in arborio rice, stirring often until the rice is golden brown and slightly toasted, about 2 minutes. Add ¼ cup (59 ml) of vegetable broth to the pot and stir until no more broth remains. Continue to do this until you have added 1½ cups (355 ml) of broth.

Add the asparagus. Stir until slightly softened. Add a ½ cup (118 ml) of vegetable broth, stirring until absorbed, and then add another. Continue to add the broth, ¼–½ cup (59–118 ml) at a time until the rice is al dente. Watch the rice carefully; you might not use all the broth.

Stir in the tomatoes, peas, nutritional yeast and cooked vegetables. Stir until combined, then reduce heat to low and keep warm. If risotto becomes too thick, add in another ¼–½ cup (59–118 ml) vegetable broth.

Make the Pea Coulis. In a food processor, mix together peas, garlic, mint, basil, olive oil, and white wine vinegar. Stir ½ cup (118 ml) of the pea coulis to the risotto mixture.

Make the Pea Shoot Salad. Toss together pea shoots, olive oil, white balsamic vinegar and a pinch each of salt and pepper.

To serve: Divide the risotto among 6-8 bowls. Top with a dollop of pea coulis and a small mound of the pea shoot salad. Serve immediately.

*See photo on page 88.

BUTTERNUT SQUASH RISOTTO

— SERVES 4 —

This risotto might be one of the creamiest dishes I've ever created, and it's completely vegan. Basically, you are making a butternut squash puree to add into the risotto as it cooks. I've never understood the fuss about making risotto. Sure, it takes a little bit of hands-on time, but the constant stirring is like meditation to me. I put on a podcast, pour myself a glass of wine and enjoy standing over the stove, creating a warm bowl of comfort. Thirty minutes later, you are rewarded with a rich, luxurious risotto dish without any cream or butter.

Cooking spray (if needed)

3 cups (440 g) butternut squash, peeled and cubed

1 medium white or yellow onion, chopped

2 garlic cloves, chopped

¼ tsp crushed red pepper flakes

Salt and freshly ground black pepper

2 cups (475 ml) vegetable broth

4 tsp (20 ml) extra virgin olive oil, divided

8 fresh sage leaves, chopped

1 tbsp (10 g) nutritional yeast

1½–2 cups (350–475 ml) water

1 cup (210 g) arborio rice

Heat a large nonstick skillet over medium heat and lightly spray with cooking spray, if needed. Add the butternut squash, onion, garlic and crushed red pepper flakes. Season with salt and pepper and cook, stirring occasionally, until the onion is translucent, about 10 minutes.

Add the vegetable broth to the skillet and bring mixture to a boil, then reduce heat to low and simmer until squash is tender, about 15 minutes.

While the squash is cooking, make the fried sage. Heat 1 teaspoon olive oil in a small sauté pan over medium heat and add the sage leaves. Cook until lightly fried, crispy but not burnt. Remove and set aside.

Place the squash mixture in a high-powered blender along with the nutritional yeast and puree until very smooth and creamy. It will be somewhat thick.

Add the squash mixture to a medium saucepan along with water to thin. It should be the consistency of vegetable broth.

In a separate saucepan, heat 1 tablespoon (15 ml) olive oil over medium heat. Add the rice and cook for 1-2 minutes until toasted and golden brown. A ladle at a time (about ½ cup [118 ml]), add in the butternut broth and cook, stirring often, until the broth is absorbed. Continue, ½ cup (118 ml) at a time, until the rice is creamy and cooked through. The entire process should take roughly 25–30 minutes. You may not use all of the broth.

Serve immediately and garnish with fried sage.

SUMMER FARRO SALAD

— SERVES 6–8 —

This is my Italian version of tabbouleh, a Middle Eastern dish made with cracked wheat, tomatoes, lots of herbs and fresh lemon dressing. This similar salad features nutty farro, thinly sliced cucumbers and a slightly sweet maple dressing.

It's a fairly simple recipe that manages to pack in lots of flavor; substantial enough on its own, it's also lovely as a side dish, especially with homemade veggie burgers. Like any good grain salad, this one is adaptable to your taste, so don't be afraid to use what you have in your fridge. Crumbled goat cheese or feta would work instead of ricotta salata, as does any mixture of herbs. Just don't skimp on the amounts— you want the fresh herbs to shine through in every bite.

1 cup (140 g) uncooked farro

2 cups (195 g) English cucumber, peeled, seeded and sliced thin

2 cups (360 g) cherry tomatoes, halved

½ cup (5 g) fresh basil, chopped

½ cup (15 g) fresh parsley, chopped

DRESSING

1 tbsp (15 ml) red wine vinegar

1 tbsp (15 ml) pure maple syrup

3 tbsp (45 ml) extra virgin olive oil

½ tsp salt

¼ tsp freshly ground black pepper

½ cup (65 g) ricotta salata, crumbled

Rinse and drain the farro. Place in a medium-sized pot and add enough water to cover the farro. Bring farro to a boil, then reduce heat to medium low and simmer for 30 minutes. Drain of any excess water and let cool.

Place in a medium bowl and toss with cucumbers, tomatoes, basil and parsley. In a separate small bowl, whisk together the red wine vinegar, maple syrup, olive oil, salt and pepper. Toss dressing with farro and let sit for 10 minutes to marinate. Add in crumbled ricotta salata and serve.

VEGAN VERSION: Omit the ricotta salata.

BRUNCH POLENTA

— SERVES 4 —

I just recently got into the habit of topping my salads, pizza and polenta bowl with a freshly poached egg. It's a fancy way to add in more protein, and the silky yolk tastes great stirred into cheesy polenta. If you had a few-too-many glasses of wine the night before, nothing cures a hangover quite like this brunch polenta.

1 cup (150 g) cornmeal

4 cups (960 ml) water

Salt and freshly ground black pepper

¾ cup (70 g) shredded cheddar cheese

1 tbsp (15 g) butter

1 tbsp (15 ml) extra virgin olive oil

1 shallot, chopped

2 garlic cloves, chopped

4 cups (270 g) kale leaves or baby spinach leaves, finely chopped

4 large eggs

1 tbsp (15 ml) white vinegar

Make the polenta: Whisk together the cornmeal, water and a generous pinch each of salt and pepper in a medium saucepan over medium heat. Continue to stir often until polenta is cooked through and creamy, about 10–15 minutes. Reduce heat to low and stir in the cheddar cheese and butter.

While the polenta is cooking, heat the olive oil in a large skillet over medium heat and add the shallot and garlic. Cook until soft, about 1–2 minutes. Season with a pinch each of salt and pepper. Add in the kale leaves or spinach and cook until just wilted, about 4–5 minutes. Reduce heat to low and set aside.

Place 5 cups (1.2 L) of water in a medium saucepan and bring to a boil. Reduce heat to a simmer and add in the vinegar.

Crack the eggs individually into a ramekin or cup. Create a gentle whirlpool with your spoon in the water to help the egg white wrap around the yolk. Slowly tip the egg into the water, white first. Leave to cook for 3 minutes. Remove with a slotted spoon, and drain on a paper towel. This prevents the egg water from getting onto the polenta, making it overly soggy.

Divide the polenta into 4 bowls along with the cooked kale. Add 1 poached egg to each bowl along with a pinch of pepper. Serve immediately.

WHITE WINE RISOTTO WITH MUSHROOMS AND LEEKS

— SERVES 4-6 —

It's fancy food for the plant-based crowd. Sautéed leeks and mushrooms are a welcome pairing for tender arborio rice. To mimic the intense umami of Parmesan cheese, dissolve nutritional yeast into the broth before ladling into the risotto. This will ensure a deep, savory flavor in every bite.

2 tbsp (30 ml) extra virgin olive oil, divided

1 cup (90 g) leeks, chopped

8 oz (225 g) mushrooms, chopped

4 cups (960 ml) low-sodium vegetable broth

2 tbsp (20 g) nutritional yeast

1 cup (185 g) arborio rice

½ cup (120 ml) white wine

½ tsp dried thyme

¼ tsp crushed red pepper flakes

Salt and freshly ground black pepper

¼ cup (5 g) fresh parsley, chopped

Heat 1 tablespoon (15 ml) olive oil over medium heat in a medium saucepan. Add the leeks and mushrooms and cook until leeks are reduced and mushrooms are lightly browned, about 8–10 minutes. Remove from the pan and set aside.

Combine the vegetable broth and nutritional yeast in the same saucepan and simmer over low heat.

Heat the remaining tablespoon (15 ml) of olive oil in a separate saucepan and add the arborio rice. Cook for 1–2 minutes until just toasted and add in the white wine, thyme and crushed red pepper flakes. Cook, stirring often, until all the liquid is absorbed. Add in the vegetable broth, a ladle (about ½ cup [118 ml]) at a time, and cook, stirring often, until the broth is absorbed. Continue, ½ cup (118 ml) at a time until the rice is creamy and cooked through. The entire process should take roughly 20 minutes. You may not use all of the broth.

Just before the risotto is finished, add back in the mushroom and leek mixture and cook another 5 minutes until risotto is creamy. Season to taste with salt and pepper. Depending on how salty your broth is, you may not need any additional salt. Just before serving, mix in the parsley.

yes! you can have bread (and pasta salad)

I'd like to challenge the notion that salads are boring, basic and unsatisfying. With added grains and/or protein, salads become meal worthy. Let me be clear. There's no rule that says you can't enjoy bread, pasta or grains. With a healthy addition of fruits and vegetables, these salads become balanced, healthy picks.

Pack the Simple Summer Pasta Salad (page 121) or Balsamic and Basil Pasta Salad (page 109) for potlucks and enjoy the Cherry, Strawberry and Balsamic Panzanella Salad (page 111) on a warm summer day. For a holiday-inspired treat, don't miss the Thanksgiving Panzanella Salad (page 112) filled with cornbread croutons, kale, roasted butternut squash and a tangy maple dressing.

BALSAMIC AND BASIL PASTA SALAD

— SERVES 6–8 —

This pasta salad is built to impress. I've made this dairy-free dish for countless potlucks and it's a hit time after time. The secret is the fragrant, balsamic basil dressing that highlights the assortment of roasted vegetables. Once you've tried it here, enjoy the aromatic dressing on tomatoes and grilled eggplant. The other beauty of this pasta salad is that it only gets better with time. Make it in the morning and serve it at room temperature in the afternoon as a hearty side salad or main dish.

1½ cups (195 g) yellow squash, sliced into half-moons

1½ cups (185 g) zucchini, sliced into half-moons

1 cup (80 g) eggplant, roughly chopped

1 cup (150 g) red bell pepper, roughly chopped

1 tbsp (15 ml) extra virgin olive oil

Salt and freshly ground black pepper

1 lb (455 g) whole-wheat orecchiette pasta (or penne or shells)

BALSAMIC DRESSING

1 clove garlic, minced

½ cup (10 g) fresh basil, minced, packed

¼ cup (60 ml) balsamic vinegar

4 tbsp and 1 tsp (64 ml) extra virgin olive oil

Salt and freshly ground black pepper

Preheat oven to 400°F (204°C).

Toss the squash, zucchini, eggplant and red bell pepper with 1 tablespoon (15 ml) olive oil and a large pinch each of salt and pepper. Place in a glass baking dish and roast for 35–40 minutes until tender.

While the vegetables are roasting, cook the pasta. Heat a large pot of salted water to boiling and add the pasta. Cook until al dente. Remove and toss with water to stop the cooking and prevent the noodles from sticking together. Drain completely.

Make the dressing. Whisk together the garlic, basil, balsamic and olive oil. Season with a pinch each of salt and pepper. Remove the vegetables from the oven and let cool until warm but not piping hot.

Toss together the vegetables, pasta and dressing. Season to taste with more salt and pepper if needed. Enjoy as is or at room temperature.

ITALIAN NIÇOISE SALAD

— SERVES 4-6 —

Salad niçoise gets an Italian makeover in this simple dinner or picnic salad. While there seem to be a lot of steps, you are basically using the same pot of salted water to cook the vegetables and pasta—first the green beans, then the potatoes, then the pennette. Doing this allows each ingredient to be finished just as it becomes tender, preventing overcooked beans or mushy potatoes.

When I am using a small number of olives in a dish, I will forgo the jars and head to the fresh olive bar at the grocery store instead. I can find a wider variety of olives there and it's usually less expensive to just buy exactly what I need.

1 lb (455 g) haricots verts (thin green beans), trimmed, halved width-wise

2 medium red potatoes, diced

1½ cups (160 g) pennette pasta (can substitute other small pasta shape)

DRESSING

⅓ cup (80 ml) fresh lemon juice

2 cloves garlic, minced

⅓ cup (80 ml) extra virgin olive oil

1 tsp dried oregano

Salt and freshly ground black pepper

1 pint (300 g) cherry tomatoes, halved

⅓ cup (60 g) niçoise olives, halved (can substitute kalamata olives)

⅓ cup (5 g) fresh basil, chopped

¼ cup (5 g) fresh parsley leaves, chopped

Salt and freshly ground black pepper to taste

Bring a large pot of salted water to a boil. Once the water boils, add in the green beans and cook until just crisp-tender, about 3–4 minutes. Using tongs or a slotted spoon, remove the green beans and place in a bowl of ice water until cool to the touch. Drain the beans and set aside. Keep the bowl of ice water, adding in more ice for the potatoes.

Bring the remaining water back to a boil. Add the potatoes and cook until they are tender, about 10 minutes. Using tongs or a slotted spoon, remove the potatoes and place in the ice water bowl until cool to the touch. Drain the potatoes and set aside.

Bring the remaining water back to a boil and add in the pennette. Cook until al dente per the package directions. Drain the pasta but do not rinse, set aside.

Whisk together the lemon juice, minced garlic cloves, olive oil, oregano and a pinch of salt and pepper. Place the beans, potatoes, pennette, tomatoes, olives, basil and parsley into a large bowl and gently toss together. Drizzle in the dressing and toss. Season to taste with salt and pepper, if needed.

CHERRY, STRAWBERRY AND BALSAMIC PANZANELLA SALAD

— SERVES 4–6 —

If there's one panzanella salad you make, I hope it's this one—a beautiful assortment of fresh summer berries tossed in a reduced balsamic vinegar dressing with crispy, crunchy bread. Swoon! It's summer perfection in a salad. To make this salad vegetarian, stir in some feta cheese at the end. Totally optional, but the creamy tang of feta pairs perfectly with the tart cherries.

½ cup (120 ml) balsamic vinegar

2 tbsp (30 g) packed brown sugar

3 cups (280 g) crusty bread, cubed

¼ cup (5 g) fresh basil, chopped into bite-size pieces, plus extra for garnish

1 cup (225 g) fresh cherries, halved and pitted

1 cup (145 g) fresh strawberries, sliced

¼ cup (25 g) almonds, chopped and toasted

⅓ cup (80 ml) extra virgin olive oil

Salt and freshly ground black pepper

Stir balsamic vinegar and brown sugar together in a small saucepan over medium heat. Bring to a gentle boil, then reduce heat to medium-low and cook until reduced by ½, about 10 minutes. Set aside and let cool.

In a large bowl, toss together the crusty bread cubes, basil, cherries, strawberries and almonds. Drizzle with cooled balsamic vinegar, olive oil and salt and pepper. Gently toss to combine and serve garnished with additional basil.

VEGAN VERSION: Replace the bread with vegan bread, same amount.

THANKSGIVING PANZANELLA SALAD

— SERVES 6–8, OR MORE WITH SMALLER PORTIONS —

You can use any prepared cornbread for this recipe. I like to make this salad a day or two after I make cornbread so that the bread is slightly hard and better soaks up the wonderful maple-Dijon dressing. If you're using fresh cornbread, place it in the oven to toast before tossing with the rest of the ingredients.

1 medium butternut squash, cubed into 1-inch (2.5-cm) pieces (about 4 cups [560 g])

1 tsp extra virgin olive oil

¼ tsp salt

¼ tsp freshly ground black pepper

6 cups (520 g) cornbread, cut into 1-inch (2.5-cm) cubes

8 cups (536 g) kale leaves

DRESSING

2 tsp (10 ml) Dijon mustard

2 tbsp (30 ml) pure maple syrup

1 tbsp (15 ml) apple cider vinegar

1 clove garlic, minced

Salt and freshly ground black pepper

⅓ cup (80 ml) extra virgin olive oil

Preheat oven to 400°F (204°C).

Toss squash with olive oil, salt and pepper, then place on a baking sheet in a single layer. Roast for 30 minutes until just tender. Remove from oven and set aside.

If using fresh cornbread, place cubes in a single layer on a baking sheet and place into the 400°F (204°C) oven. Bake for 5 minutes until cornbread is just toasted through.

Finely shred the kale leaves. Remove the stems and stack the leaves on top of one another. Tightly roll like a cigar. Using a sharp knife, start from the end and slice into ¼–½-inch (0.5–1-cm) ribbons of kale leaves. Place the kale into a large bowl.

Whisk together the mustard, maple syrup, apple cider vinegar, garlic and a pinch each of salt and pepper. Slowly whisk in the olive oil until the dressing is creamy and thick. Toss dressing over the kale and massage into the kale leaves. Add in the roasted squash and cornbread. Toss to combine. I enjoy this best at room temperature, but you can also serve it cold.

VEGAN VERSION: Replace the cornbread with vegan cornbread, same amount.

SICILIAN KALE SALAD WITH ORZO

— SERVES 4 —

This inspiration for this dish comes from one of my favorite ways to eat kale: lightly sautéed and topped with raisins, balsamic vinegar and toasted pine nuts. I know it sounds a little strange, but the combination of hearty kale with tart raisins and slightly sweet balsamic vinegar is heavenly. To make this more of a meal, I add in cooked orzo and top with a generous shaving of Parmesan cheese.

Tuscan kale, also called lacinato, dinosaur or black kale, is the best type of kale to use here. Its crinkled leaves are smaller and more tender than the leaves of curly kale.

1 cup (200 g) orzo pasta

1 tbsp (15 ml) extra virgin olive oil

1 large bunch kale, preferably Tuscan (black) kale, stems removed, leaves torn into bite-sized pieces

2 cloves garlic, minced

¼ cup (40 g) raisins

⅛ cup (30 ml) balsamic vinegar

¼ cup (40 g) pine nuts, toasted

Salt and freshly ground black pepper

¼ cup (25 g) Parmesan cheese, freshly shaved

Make the pasta. Bring a large pot of salted water to a boil. Add the orzo, reduce heat to medium-low and cook until al dente, about 8–9 minutes. While the pasta is cooking, make the sauce. Drain and set aside.

Heat the olive oil in a large saucepan over medium high heat and add the kale. Cook for 3–4 minutes, until just wilted. Add in the finely minced garlic, it should melt when warmed with the kale. Remove from heat and stir in the raisins, balsamic vinegar, toasted pine nuts and salt/pepper to taste.

Toss with the orzo pasta and stir in the Parmesan cheese.

VEGAN VERSION: Replace Parmesan Cheese with Vegan Parmesan Cheese (page 182), same amount.

ALL HAIL KALE CAESAR SALAD

— SERVES 6 AS A SIDE DISH —

This simple kale Caesar is one of my go-to recipes when I know I need to eat a lot of hearty greens, but want cheese instead. I've made this for dozens of cooking classes and it's a hit every time—even with people who think they don't like kale. The secret is slicing the kale very thinly and massaging the dressing into the kale leaves before adding the rest of the ingredients. If you have it on hand, add a heaping teaspoon of white miso to the dressing to give it the umami that you would find in a traditional Caesar dressing. It's also great without the miso. Since I'm a huge crouton aficionado, I want to enjoy the flavor of croutons in every bite. Therefore, I'm using bread crumbs instead of croutons so that every kale leaf gets coated in crunchy goodness.

1 large bunch Tuscan kale (a.k.a. black or dinosaur kale)

CAESAR DRESSING

1 lemon, juiced and zested

2 cloves garlic

⅛–¼ tsp crushed red pepper flakes (for a spicier salad, use ¼ tsp)

1 tsp white miso (optional)

3 tbsp (45 ml) extra virgin olive oil

Salt and freshly ground black pepper

⅛–¼ cup (25–45 g) Parmesan cheese, freshly grated

⅛–¼ cup (15–30 g) good-quality bread crumbs

Salt and freshly ground black pepper

Rinse and pat dry kale leaves. Remove any tough stems and stack leaves on top of one another and roll up tightly like a cigar. Starting at the end, thinly slice "ribbons" of kale, like a wide chiffonade and set aside in a large bowl.

Combine the lemon juice and zest, minced garlic cloves, crushed red pepper and miso together in a small bowl and whisk until miso is dissolved and combined. Slowly whisk in the olive oil and season with a generous pinch of salt and freshly ground black pepper.

Toss the dressing over the kale and using your hands, gently massage the dressing into the kale leaves. This method allows the kale to become very tender and allows you to use less dressing than you normally would on such a large kale salad. After massaging for 3-4 minutes, toss in the cheese and bread crumbs. Start with ⅛ cup (15 g) each and then add more if needed. Season to taste, if needed, with salt and pepper.

To make this more of a meal, add in chopped hard-boiled eggs and a can of drained and rinsed garbanzo beans. If going this route, increase the dressing by half.

NOTE: Since I am using raw garlic here, I like to make a garlic paste before adding to the dressing so that no one gets a hunk of raw garlic when they go to take a bite! To do this, thinly mince the garlic and place into a pile on a cutting board. Using the back of a large knife, press the minced garlic down and scrape until a paste forms. Then, add to the dressing bowl.

VEGAN VERSION: Replace bread crumbs with vegan bread crumbs, same amount. Replace Parmesan cheese with Vegan Parmesan Cheese (page 182), same amount.

COUSCOUS, ARUGULA AND MUSHROOM SALAD

— SERVES 4 —

Arugula with onions and thinly sliced mushrooms is one of my favorite salad combinations. While I try to eat at least one salad a day to ensure I am getting as many vegetables as possible, it can be difficult when I am on the go or craving a heartier meal. Therefore, I've taken my simple salad and added cooked Israeli couscous and kidney beans, transforming a light meal into a satisfying lunch or dinner. The toothy bite of large Israeli couscous stands up beautifully to the assertive arugula and creamy kidney beans.

This salad also tastes great the next day, as the vinaigrette has more time to seep into the couscous, beans and vegetables. To prepare in advance, make as directed but don't add the arugula until just before serving.

2 tsp (10 ml) extra virgin olive oil

1 cup (150 g) Israeli couscous

2 cups (473 ml) water

Salt and freshly ground black pepper

DRESSING

¼ cup (60 ml) extra virgin olive oil

⅛ cup (30 ml) red wine vinegar

2 tbsp (30 ml) balsamic vinegar

1 tsp smoked paprika

1 tsp dried oregano

2 cloves garlic, minced

10 oz (285 g) cremini or white mushrooms, thinly sliced

1 (15-oz [425-g]) can red kidney beans, drained and rinsed

½ cup (55 g) red onion, halved and thinly sliced

2 cups (60 g) packed arugula leaves, chopped into bite-sized pieces (see note)

Place 2 teaspoons (10 ml) olive oil in a saucepan over medium heat. Add the couscous and cook, stirring, until toasted and light golden brown, about 5 minutes. Add water, season with a pinch each of salt and pepper and bring to a boil. Reduce the heat to a simmer, cover and cook until the liquid is absorbed, about 8–10 minutes.

Make the dressing. Whisk together olive oil, red wine vinegar, balsamic vinegar, paprika, oregano, garlic and a pinch each of salt and pepper. Place the dressing in a bowl and add the mushrooms, beans and red onion and let marinate for 15 minutes.

Stir in the cooked couscous and arugula and place in the fridge to let marinate for at least another 30 minutes. Season to taste with salt and pepper. Like most chilled salads, the longer this sits, the better is gets. If making the day before, add all the ingredients except the arugula.

NOTE: I love the peppery bite of arugula, but if you prefer a milder flavor, sub in chopped spinach leaves.

TORTELLINI PASTA SALAD

— SERVES 4-6 —

Roasted broccoli, asparagus, tomatoes and cheese tortellini tossed with a fresh lemon–olive oil dressing make a perfect salad for family potlucks or lazy afternoons with friends. Prepare this ahead of time and serve at room temperature.

2 cups (109 g) broccoli florets, chopped

2 cups (200 g) asparagus, chopped

1 tsp extra virgin olive oil

Salt and freshly ground black pepper

9 oz (255 g) fresh cheese tortellini

2 cups (272 g) tomatoes, chopped, or cherry tomatoes, halved

DRESSING

2 tbsp (30ml) fresh lemon juice

1 clove garlic, minced

¼ cup (60 ml) extra virgin olive oil

½ tsp salt

¼ tsp freshly ground black pepper

Preheat oven to 400°F (204°C). Toss the broccoli and asparagus with 1 teaspoon olive oil along with a pinch each of salt and pepper. Place in a single layer on a baking sheet and roast for 20–25 minutes until tender. Remove from oven and set aside.

While the vegetables are roasting, make the pasta. Bring a large pot of water to a boil and add in the tortellini. Cook, according to package directions, until tender. When tortellini rise to the top of the water, remove them with a slotted spoon and place in a large bowl and let cool to room temperature.

Add the roasted vegetables and tomatoes to the bowl along with the cooked tortellini. Whisk together the lemon juice, garlic, olive oil, salt and pepper. Drizzle over the tortellini and toss together. Season to taste with salt and pepper and serve at room temperature or chilled.

SIMPLE SUMMER PASTA SALAD (ITALIAN FLAG SALAD)

— SERVES 4-6 —

Don't be fooled by the simple ingredient list—this salad is bright, flavorful and a must-make for cookouts and picnics throughout the summer. This is one of the first pasta salads I ever made. Though I love the combination of vegetables here, it's easily adapted to whatever you have on hand.

The secret to this salad is infusing the serving bowl with garlic, providing a delicate background essence of flavor in every bite. The ingredients will pick up the garlic juices in the bowl, coating every bite with a subtle dose of sweet, garlicky flavor. Enjoy this one warm or at room temperature.

3 cups (330 g) green beans, trimmed, halved if long

8 oz (225 g) mini penne or other small pasta

2 garlic cloves, 1 whole, 1 minced

2 beefsteak tomatoes, chopped

½ cup (10 g) fresh basil, finely chopped

½ cup (15 g) fresh parsley leaves, finely chopped

3 tbsp (45 ml) extra version olive oil

1 large lemon, juiced

Salt and freshly ground black pepper

Bring a large pot of water fitted with a steamer basket to a boil. Add the green beans and steam until bright green and just tender, about 5 minutes. Remove the steamer basket and add more water if needed.

Add in the mini penne and cook until just al dente according to package directions.

While the pasta is cooking, cut the whole garlic clove in half and rub both halves on the the inside of the serving bowl. The clove will slowly melt into the side of the bowl, infusing garlic oil into the finished dish.

Add the steamed green beans, cooked penne, chopped tomatoes, basil, parsley and minced garlic clove into the prepared bowl. Drizzle with olive oil, lemon juice and a generous pinch of salt and pepper. Gently toss together. The heat of the pasta will melt the garlic on the side of the bowl along with the vegetables. Season to taste.

Serve as is or place in the fridge for up to 2 days.

GRILLED RATATOUILLE PANZANELLA SALAD WITH BASIL DRESSING

— SERVES 6–8 AS A SIDE DISH —

As a vegetarian, I tend to immediately pass over anything on the menu that contains the words "roasted vegetables." Even though I love them in my own house, restaurants tend to include the lowly roasted vegetable sandwich on their menu as a de facto meatless option. It's often a flavorless, soggy choice. This salad is my attempt to remake the roasted vegetable sandwich into a vibrant, summer salad option with chopped grilled vegetables, toasted ciabatta cubes and a fresh basil dressing. One bite, and you'll never look at roasted vegetables the same way again.

BASIL DRESSING

1 cup (15 g) fresh basil, tightly packed

3 tbsp (45 ml) white wine vinegar (can substitute white balsamic vinegar)

2 tsp (10 g) sugar

1 clove garlic

1 tsp Dijon mustard

⅓ cup (80 ml) extra virgin olive oil

Salt and freshly ground black pepper

1 medium Italian eggplant, sliced into 1-inch (2.5-cm) thick lengthwise slices

1 medium red onion, sliced into 2-inch (5-cm) slices

1 red bell pepper

1 yellow squash, halved lengthwise

1 zucchini, halved lengthwise

2 tbsp (30 ml) extra virgin olive oil, or enough to brush vegetables

1 pint (300 g) cherry tomatoes

½ loaf ciabatta, split in half horizontally

Place the basil, vinegar, sugar, garlic and mustard in a food processor or blender. Puree mixture until smooth and bright green. Keep the motor running and drizzle in the olive oil until creamy and blended. Season with a pinch each of salt and pepper.

Lightly brush the eggplant, onion, pepper, squash and zucchini with olive oil on all sides.

Place the zucchini, squash, eggplant and onion slices on a grill or grill-pan over medium heat, cut-side down. Grill until vegetables are slightly charred, then flip to cook the other side. Cook until tender, about 3–5 more minutes. Remove the vegetables and transfer to a cutting board. Coarsely chop, then place in a large bowl.

Add the pepper to the grill or grill pan and cook, turning occasionally, until charred all over and tender, about 12–15 minutes. Remove the pepper, place in a bowl and cover with a kitchen towel to let steam for 10 minutes. Remove the stem and peel, then seed and chop the bell pepper into chunks. Place in the vegetable bowl.

Put the tomatoes in a grill basket or directly onto the grill pan and grill, covered, shaking occasionally, until tomatoes are charred and almost bursting, about 5 minutes. Remove and add to the vegetable bowl.

Place the ciabatta, cut-side down, onto the grill or grill pan until toasted, about 3 minutes. Flip and grill the other side. Transfer to the cutting board, slice into 2-inch (5-cm) pieces and add to the vegetable bowl. Add the dressing and toss well to combine. Season to taste with salt and pepper.

VEGAN VERSION: Replace the ciabatta with vegan bread, same amount.

BROCCOLI ORZO SALAD

— SERVES 4 —

This simple picnic salad combines three of my favorite foods: pasta, broccoli and chickpeas. Easy and delicious, this is one of my niece's most beloved summer dinners. Tossed in a simple lemon dressing with crumbled ricotta salata, it's a great choice to pack for lunch and potlucks.

1 cup (170 g) orzo

2 cups (110 g) broccoli florets, cut into bite-sized pieces

1 cup (200 g) chickpeas, cooked or, if canned, drained and rinsed

2 tbsp (30 ml) extra virgin olive oil

1 tbsp (15 ml) fresh lemon juice

Salt and freshly ground pepper

½ cup (65 g) ricotta salata, freshly crumbled

Bring a large pot of water to a boil. Add the orzo and cook until al dente according to package directions. Drain, set aside and let cool to room temperature.

While the water is boiling, steam the broccoli. For cleanup ease, I place a steamer basket on the boiling water pot and add the broccoli while the pasta cooks. Steam until bright green, about 2–3 minutes. Remove and set aside.

Toss together the cooled orzo, steamed broccoli and chickpeas. Whisk together the olive oil, lemon juice and a pinch each of salt and pepper and toss with the orzo. Gently fold in the ricotta salata and serve.

skinny soups and stews

Soups are one of the first meals I learned how to prepare, and my go-to when I have produce scraps lying around. You almost don't need a recipe, just a sauté of aromatics, a legume of choice and vegetable broth; it's a low-key way to cook without the fear of messing up.

Many of the soups here are main course items, including the White Bean, Tortellini and Kale Soup (page 138) and Pasta e Ceci (page 129). Enjoy the Italian Wonton Soup (page 130) or Zuppa di Pomodoro (page 135) as a first course or paired with a salad and bread for a full meal. I'll often make a pot of soup on Sunday to enjoy as lunch or eat as leftovers throughout the week.

PASTA E CECI

— SERVES 6-8 —

This rustic recipe is similar to Pasta e Fagioli (page 143), using ceci (chickpeas) instead of cannellini beans. For a cost-saving dinner, my mom would make this stew with whatever remnants of broken pasta she had in the pantry, creating a mixture of flavors and textures along with the creamy chickpeas. To simplify things, I call for ditalini pasta, a tiny, tubular shape used in Italian soups. Of course, any combination of small pasta shapes will work.

1 tbsp (15 ml) extra virgin olive oil

1 medium white or yellow onion, chopped

2 cloves garlic, minced

¾ tsp dried rosemary or 4–5 sprigs fresh rosemary, stems removed, leaves chopped

1 tsp dried oregano

salt and freshly ground black pepper

1 (14½-oz [410-g]) can diced tomatoes

1 (15½-oz [435-g]) can chickpeas, rinsed and drained

4 cups (950 ml) vegetable broth (use low-sodium if preferred)

1 cup (240 ml) water

¾ cup (170 g) ditalini pasta

¼ cup (25 g) Parmesan cheese, freshly grated

¼ cup (5 g) fresh parsley leaves, chopped

Heat the oil in a large soup pot or Dutch oven over medium heat. Add the onion and cook until translucent, about 5–6 minutes. Stir in the garlic, rosemary, oregano and a generous pinch each of salt and pepper. Cook for 30 seconds. Add the tomatoes with the juice to the pot and stir together. Cook for 5 minutes, stirring often, until slightly reduced.

Add the drained chickpeas to the pot and lightly mash, using a potato masher or wooden spoon. This will help to thicken the soup, making it feel more like a stew instead of a bean soup.

Add the broth and water and bring to a boil. Add in the uncooked pasta and cook for an additional 10 minutes, stirring occasionally, until just al dente. The longer the pasta cooks, the thicker the soup and the more tender the pasta will become.

Remove from heat and stir in Parmesan cheese and parsley.

NOTE: If you don't have a potato masher, you can mash the beans in advance in a food processor or by placing in a bowl and mashing with a fork.

VEGAN VERSION: Replace Parmesan cheese with Vegan Parmesan Cheese (page 182), same amount.

ITALIAN WONTON SOUP

— SERVES 4 —

This is my version of Italian wonton soup: a deeply rich mushroom broth studded with tender tortellini dumplings. The broth is so flavorful, you almost don't need the tortellini—almost! To serve, place a scoop of cooked tortellini in the bottom of a mug or cup and fill with hot, steaming broth. It's a beautiful first course or light lunch. To make this more of a meal, add your favorite chopped vegetables to the broth.

To cut down on prep, the broth can be made ahead of time and frozen.

⅔ cup (45 g) dried porcini mushrooms, rinsed

1 clove garlic, smashed

1 white or yellow onion, roughly chopped into 6–8 pieces

2 celery stalks, roughly chopped

1 carrot, roughly chopped into 4–5 pieces

2 sprigs fresh thyme or 1 tsp dried thyme

Small handful of fresh parsley, about 7–8 sprigs

1 tsp whole black peppercorns

1 tsp salt, plus more to taste

8 cups (1.9 L) water

Freshly ground black pepper

9 oz (255 g) fresh cheese tortellini

Parmesan cheese, freshly grated, for garnish

Fresh parsley leaves, chopped, for garnish

Place the mushrooms, garlic, onion, celery, carrot, thyme, parsley, peppercorns, 1 teaspoon salt and water in a large stock pot. Bring to a boil, then reduce heat to low, partially cover and cook for roughly 1 hour until broth is reduced by ½ and is dark brown. Strain the broth through a fine mesh sieve or colander. Wipe out the used pot, place the broth back in and bring to a simmer while you cook the tortellini. Season to taste, adding extra salt and pepper if needed.

Bring a medium pot of salted water to a boil. Add the tortellini and cook until tender. They should float to the top as they finish cooking so you can scoop them up and into a separate bowl.

Divide the tortellini among 4 bowls and top with mushroom broth. Garnish with parsley and Parmesan cheese, if desired. Serve hot.

RIBOLLITA TOSCANA
(TUSCAN BREAD SOUP)

— SERVES 6–8 —

Ribollita, literally translated as "reboiled," is a Tuscan potage made with leftover bread,
vegetables and white beans. Like many of the soups in this chapter, it relies
on pantry ingredients to create an inexpensive, healthy meal.

I often find myself making this stew after an indulgent dinner party, where I am left with at least
one loaf of unused bread and a produce drawer full of vegetable odds and ends. First-timers,
use this recipe as a guide so you know what the end result should look and taste like.
From there, feel free to sub in any vegetable and bean combination you prefer.

The bread cubes should be almost stale and crispy on all outside edges. If you are making this with fresh
bread, toast the cubes first to resemble croutons. To do so, place bread cubes in a single layer on a baking
sheet and toast for 5 to 10 minutes, turning once, in a 350°F (176°C) oven until golden brown and crispy.

1 tbsp (15 ml) extra virgin olive oil

4 large cloves garlic, minced

1 medium white or yellow onion, chopped

2 medium carrots, peeled and chopped

2 large celery ribs, chopped

½ tsp crushed red pepper flakes, or to taste

1 dried bay leaf

Salt and freshly ground black pepper

1 large bunch Tuscan Kale, stems removed, leaves torn into bite-sized pieces

1 (15½-oz [435-g]) can cannellini beans with liquid

6 cups (1.4 L) vegetable broth

1 (28-oz [794-g]) can whole tomatoes, drained and chopped

3 cups (105 g) day-old bread, torn into pieces

¼ cup (7 g) fresh basil, chopped

1 tbsp (15 ml) red wine vinegar

Parmesan cheese, freshly grated, to garnish

Heat the oil in a soup pot or Dutch oven over medium-high heat. Add in the garlic, onion, carrots, celery, crushed red pepper flakes and bay leaf along with a pinch each of salt and pepper. Sauté until vegetables are tender and onion is translucent, about 5–7 minutes. Add in the kale and cook another 3–4 minutes until kale is softened.

Add beans with liquid, vegetable broth and chopped tomatoes, and bring to a boil. Stir in 2 cups (70 g) of the bread cubes and reduce heat to a simmer. Cook until soup thickens slightly, about 8–10 minutes. Remove from heat, remove the bay leaf and stir in chopped basil and red wine vinegar.

To serve, divide soup among 6–8 bowls and top with remaining bread cubes and Parmesan.

VEGAN VERSION: Replace bread with vegan bread, same amount. Replace Parmesan cheese with Vegan Parmesan Cheese (page 182), same amount.

LENTIL AND BARLEY SOUP

— SERVES 4–6 —

Soups are one of my favorite things to prepare—they're so easy, and nothing is better on a chilly evening with homemade bread or a green salad. This nourishing tomato, lentil and barley version was a hit with both my family and recipe testers. Leftovers of this soup are incredible, and it freezes well, too.

1 tbsp (15 ml) extra virgin olive oil

1 cup (110 g) carrots, chopped

1 cup (100 g) celery, chopped

1 medium white or yellow onion, chopped

2 cloves garlic, minced

1 tsp dried basil

½ tsp dried oregano

¼ tsp dried thyme

2 bay leaves

4 cups (950 ml) vegetable broth

2 cups (475 ml) water

1 cup (190 g) green or brown lentils

½ cup (90 g) pearl barley

1 (14-oz [395-g]) can crushed tomatoes

¼ cup (5 g) fresh parsley leaves, finely chopped

2 tbsp (30 ml) red wine vinegar

¼ cup (25 g) Parmesan cheese, freshly grated

Heat the olive oil in a large soup pot over medium-high heat. Add the carrots, celery and onions. Sauté until vegetables are soft and lightly browned, about 8–10 minutes. Add the garlic, basil, oregano, thyme and bay leaves.

Stir in the broth, water, lentils and barley and bring to a boil. Reduce heat to medium-low, cover and simmer until lentils are tender, stirring occasionally, about 1 hour. Add in the tomatoes and simmer for another 10 minutes. Remove the bay leaves. Stir in the parsley, red wine vinegar and Parmesan cheese.

VEGAN VERSION: Replace Parmesan cheese with Vegan Parmesan Cheese (page 182), same amount.

ZUPPA DI POMODORO

— SERVES 4 —

This is a classic creamy tomato soup using whole, canned tomatoes in place of fresh. The richness of canned tomatoes pierces through the silky cream finish, making this easy soup so much better than any concentrate version. As with any of my recipes using heavy cream, feel free to substitute in silky Cashew Cream (page 184) for a dairy-free version.

1 tbsp (15 ml) olive oil

1 medium white or yellow onion, chopped

2 garlic cloves, minced

2 tsp (1 g) dried Italian seasoning

Salt

Crushed red pepper flakes

1 (28-oz [794-g]) can whole tomatoes with juice

3 cups (700 ml) vegetable broth

¼–½ cup (60–120 ml) heavy cream

½ cup (7 g) fresh basil, finely chopped

Heat the oil in a large soup pot over medium heat. Add the onion and sauté until soft and translucent, about 5 minutes. Add in the garlic, Italian seasoning and pinch each of salt and crushed red pepper flakes.

Add in the tomatoes and vegetable broth and bring to a boil. Reduce heat to low and simmer for 15–20 minutes.

Remove from heat and, in batches if needed, puree soup in a blender until smooth. Return to the pot and stir in the heavy cream and basil. Depending on how creamy you like your soup, start with ¼ cup (59 ml) cream and add up to ½ cup (118 ml), if desired.

VEGAN VERSION: Replace heavy cream with Cashew Cream (page 184), same amount.

PASTA AND LENTIL SOUP

— SERVES 6–8 —

With fifteen grams of fiber and eighteen grams of protein in every one-cup (237-ml) serving, lentils are one of the most satiating plant-based foods available. Usually costing around $1 per pound, lentils are one of nature's least-expensive superfoods. I turn to this rustic soup whenever I'm craving pasta, but need lentils and vegetables. While easy to prepare, the flavor is anything but simple. Pair this with crusty bread or a side salad.

1 tbsp (15 ml) extra virgin olive oil

1 medium white or yellow onion, finely chopped

Salt and freshly ground black pepper

4 cloves garlic, minced

½ tsp crushed red pepper flakes

1 tsp dried oregano

2 tbsp (35 g) tomato paste

2 cups (475 ml) vegetable broth (use low-sodium if preferred)

4 cups (960 ml) water

1 (14-oz [400-g]) can lentils, drained, or 2 cups (400 g) cooked lentils

8 oz (225 g) orecchiette pasta or other short pasta

¼ cup (5 g) fresh parsley leaves, chopped

3 cups (80 g) packed spinach leaves

Parmesan cheese, freshly grated, for garnish

Heat the olive oil over medium heat in a large stock pot. Add the onion and a pinch each of salt and pepper and cook until reduced and translucent, about 5–6 minutes. Add the garlic, crushed red pepper flakes and oregano and stir for 30 seconds.

Add in the tomato paste and cook another minute, stirring often. You want to create a thinned paste with the cooked onion, garlic and olive oil. Whisk in the vegetable broth and water and bring to a boil.

Add in the lentils and pasta and cook, stirring occasionally for 10 minutes until pasta is cooked through and tender. Just before serving, stir in the parsley and spinach. Divide into bowls and garnish with Parmesan cheese, if using. I like this with an extra pinch of freshly ground black pepper over the cheese.

NOTE: If using dry lentils, place in a saucepan and cover by 2 inches (5 cm) with cold water. Bring to a boil, reduce heat to low and let simmer for 30 minutes until lentils are tender. Drain and rinse before adding to the soup.

VEGAN VERSION: Omit Parmesan cheese garnish, or replace with Vegan Parmesan Cheese (page 182).

SIMMERED WHITE BEANS WITH CRUSTY BREAD

— SERVES 8-10 AS AN APPETIZER —

I originally created this recipe as an appetizer option for a relaxing girls' night in. Simmered white beans in a flavorful tomato sauce with plenty of crusty bread—I can't think of a better option to pair with wine and best friends. I serve this one right from the skillet, topped with feta cheese and parsley, along with a basket of toasted bread and crackers. A mix between a thick soup and a dip, it's perfect for sharing or enjoying like a stew. For a faster option, used canned beans, remove the water and cut down on the salt.

1 tbsp (15 ml) extra virgin olive oil

1 white or yellow onion, chopped

4 cloves garlic, chopped

¾ tsp crushed red pepper flakes

½ cup (118 ml) white wine

2 cups (400 g) dried cannellini beans, soaked and drained

4½ cups (1.1 L) water

2 bay leaves

1 (28-oz [795-g]) can crushed tomatoes

1 tsp salt

¾ cup (115 g) feta cheese, crumbled

¼ cup (10 g) fresh parsley, chopped

Crusty bread or crackers for serving

Heat the olive oil in a large skillet over medium heat. Add the onion and cook until translucent, about 5 minutes. Add in the garlic, crushed red pepper flakes and white wine. Reduce heat to medium low and simmer for 10 minutes until wine is almost completely absorbed. Stir in the dried beans, water and bay leaves. Bring to a boil, then reduce heat to a simmer and cook until tender, about 1 hour to 90 minutes.

Add in the can of crushed tomatoes and salt and cook another 10–15 minutes until thick. Remove bay leaves. Garnish with crumbled feta, parsley and bread.

VEGAN VERSION: Omit the feta cheese.

WHITE BEAN, TORTELLINI AND KALE SOUP

— SERVES 6–8 —

This is a heartier version of one of my favorite winter soups, Tortellini en Brodo (tortellini in broth). While I love the thought of eating just tortellini in a flavorful broth, the addition of both cannellini beans and kale make this a little more virtuous. After dishing, garnish with freshly ground black pepper and freshly grated Parmesan cheese.

1 tbsp (15 ml) extra virgin olive oil

1 small white onion, finely chopped

2 medium carrots, chopped

2 cloves garlic, finely chopped

2 (15-oz [425-g]) cans cannellini beans, rinsed and drained

7 cups (1.6 L) vegetable broth (low-sodium, if desired)

1 (14½-oz [410-g]) can fire-roasted diced tomatoes with juice

4 cups (120 g) Tuscan kale (a.k.a. black or dinosaur kale), about 1 bunch, stems removed, leaves chopped

9 oz (255 g) fresh, frozen or dried cheese tortellini

½ cup (35 g) Parmesan cheese, freshly grated, to garnish

In a large soup pot, heat the olive oil over medium heat. Add the onion, carrots and garlic and cook until the vegetables are soft, about 5 minutes, stirring occasionally.

Add in the beans, broth and diced tomatoes with juice bring to a boil over medium-high heat. Reduce heat to a simmer, add in the kale and tortellini and cook until tortellini is just tender, about 5–6 minutes.

Season with pepper and serve. Top with Parmesan cheese.

LEMON CHICKPEA SOUP

— SERVES 6 —

I know putting lemon juice in a soup sounds weird, but this simple recipe has been shared—and loved—by thousands of readers of my blog, Delish Knowledge. A one-pot soup filled with vegetables, garbanzo beans and orzo pasta, it's my chicken noodle soup for vegetarians. Finish with a generous squirt of lemon juice for a bright and bold cold-weather soup.

1 tbsp (15 ml) extra virgin olive oil

1 onion, diced

2 large carrots, halved lengthwise and finely sliced

3 celery stalks, chopped

3 garlic cloves, minced

½ tsp dried thyme

Freshly ground black pepper

6 cups (1.44 L) vegetable broth

1 cup (237 ml) water

1 (15-oz [425-g]) can chickpeas, rinsed and drained

1 small sprig rosemary

1 cup (170 g) orzo

1 bay leaf

⅛ cup (30 ml) fresh lemon juice

Heat the olive oil in a soup pot or Dutch oven over medium heat. Add the onion, carrots, celery and garlic. Cook for 5 minutes until vegetables are soft. Add the thyme and a pinch of pepper; stir together.

Add the vegetable broth and water and bring to a boil. Add the chickpeas, rosemary, orzo and bay leaf. Reduce heat to a low simmer and cook for 10 minutes until orzo is cooked through. Reduce heat to low, remove bay leaf and rosemary sprig and stir in lemon juice.

ITALIAN WEDDING SOUP

— SERVES 6 —

I've taken my family recipe and made it vegetarian friendly, thanks to brown rice and mushroom meatballs. Wedding soup (minestra maritata) is so named because greens and meat are said to go so well together. Well, in this wedding soup, greens and vegan meatballs deliciously marry together.

BROWN RICE AND MUSHROOM MEATBALLS

¾ cup (145 g) brown rice

1½ cups (355 ml) water

2 tbsp (30 ml) extra virgin olive oil, divided

1 medium white or yellow onion, finely diced

8 oz (225 g) white button mushrooms, sliced

2 cloves garlic, minced

½ cup (55 g) bread crumbs

¼ cup (30 g) whole-wheat or all-purpose flour

1 tsp dried basil

¼ tsp crushed red pepper flakes

Salt and freshly ground black pepper

1 cup (14 g) loosely packed basil leaves

1 white or yellow onion, chopped into chunks

2 stalks celery, chopped into chunks

1 carrot, chopped into large chunks

5 cloves garlic, peeled

2 tbsp (30 ml) extra virgin olive oil

64 oz (1.9 L) vegetable broth

10 oz (285 g) frozen chopped spinach, thawed

½ cup (3 oz [85 g]) acini de pepe pasta

Salt and freshly ground black pepper

Make the meatballs. Add the brown rice along with 1½ cups (355 ml) water in a small saucepan and bring to a boil. Reduce heat to low, cover and simmer for 30–40 minutes until rice is tender. Remove, drain and let cool completely.

While the rice is cooking, heat 1 tablespoon (15 ml) olive oil in a large skillet over medium heat. Add the onion and mushrooms and cook until soft and golden brown, about 10 minutes. Add the garlic and cook another minute. Remove from heat until rice is cooled.

Add the cooled brown rice, cooked onion and mushroom mixture, bread crumbs, flour, basil and crushed red pepper flakes to a food processor and pulse until the mixture just comes together. Season with salt and pepper to taste. Form the meatballs into 1-inch (2.5-cm) balls and set aside.

Heat remaining olive oil in a non-stick skillet over medium heat. Add the meatballs in batches, and cook until golden brown and crispy on all sides. Remove and set aside.

Place basil, onion, celery, carrot and garlic in a food processor and mince into a smooth paste.

Heat olive oil in a large stock pot over high heat and add the vegetable mixture. Cook for 5 minutes, stirring often, until the vegetables start to lose moisture. Add the vegetable broth, bring to a boil and then reduce to a simmer.

Remove the excess water from the thawed spinach by squeezing it through a sieve. Then add the spinach, pasta and meatballs to the pot and simmer for 10 minutes. Season to taste, if needed, with salt and pepper.

*See photo on page 127.

PASTA E FAGIOLI

— SERVES 6–8 —

I would be remiss if I didn't include my version of Pasta e Fagioli. The combination of pasta and beans, two staples of my diet, simmered in a fragrant tomato sauce makes for a satisfying, comforting soup. For an extra serving of vegetables, I stir in fresh spinach leaves at the end, leaving just enough time to wilt them in savory tomato goodness.

When I was growing up, my mom relied on two dishes to get us through any lean times: white beans with spinach and this pasta fagioli. Though we didn't want for anything, sometimes feeding a family of five was more about economics than taste or preference, hence my continued love affair with this bean and pasta soup. Pasta fagioli reminds me of home, of boisterous family dinners and my Mamma.

Whether you are looking for comfort or just a giant bowl of healthy goodness, this soup is for you. I know there are several varieties of this soup, including the one made famous by Olive Garden, but this is how my grandma makes it, how my mom makes it, and therefore, how I make it. Generations of women can't be wrong.

1 tbsp (15 ml) extra virgin olive oil

½ small white onion, chopped

Salt and freshly ground black pepper

1 tsp crushed red pepper flakes (or more for extra kick)

3 garlic cloves, minced

3–4 fresh rosemary sprigs

1 (28-oz [795-ml]) can regular, plain tomato sauce

½ cup (10 g) chopped fresh parsley leaves

2 (15-oz [425-g]) cans cannellini beans, rinsed and drained

½ lb (225 g) ditalini pasta

2 cups (60 g) spinach

In a large saucepan, heat the olive oil over medium heat. Add the chopped onion and a pinch each of salt, pepper and crushed red pepper flakes. Sauté for about 5 minutes, until onion is translucent and soft. Add in the garlic and rosemary and cook for 30 seconds, taking care not to burn the herbs or garlic. Add the tomato sauce, parsley and beans. Reduce heat to low and simmer for 1 hour.

Bring a large pot of salted water to boil over high heat. Add the ditalini pasta and cook until al dente, reserving 3 cups (708 ml) pasta water.

Before serving, add the cooked pasta to the tomato and bean sauce and thin with reserved pasta water. You will probably not use all 3 cups (708 ml). Add ½ cup (118 ml) at a time, stir, and add more if need be. Thin the tomato sauce until it resembles a soup broth. Stir in the spinach until wilted.

This tastes even better the next day. If you have leftovers, add a little more pasta water before refrigerating.

SPINACH AND WHITE BEAN SOUP

— SERVES 4–6 —

What you see is what you get with this soup, a velvety mix of creamy white beans, zucchini and plenty of spinach. Ironically, this was one of my most-hated dishes as a child, something I would beg my mom not to make, pleading for almost anything else in its place. These days, it's become a rotating favorite in my house and my go-to soup when I need a break from heavier meals.

1 tbsp (15 ml) olive oil

1 medium white or yellow onion, chopped

3 large cloves garlic, chopped

1 medium zucchini, chopped

½ tsp dried thyme

2 bay leaves

2 (15½-oz [445-g]) cans cannellini beans with liquid

4 cups (950 ml) vegetable broth

4 cups (120 g) baby spinach leaves

Parmesan cheese, freshly grated, to garnish

Heat oil in a large stock pot over medium heat. Add the onion and cook until soft and translucent, about 8 minutes. Add in garlic, zucchini and thyme and cook until zucchini is soft and lightly golden.

Add in the bay leaves, cannellini beans with liquid and vegetable broth and bring to a boil. Reduce heat to medium and simmer, about 10 minutes. Stir in the spinach until wilted, remove bay leaves, sprinkle with Parmesan cheese and serve immediately.

VEGAN VERSION: Omit Parmesan cheese or replace with Vegan Parmesan Cheese (page 182), same amount.

WEEKNIGHT NOODLE SOUP

— SERVES 6 —

This weeknight noodle soup is a favorite in my house season after season. It's simple and restorative, packed with vegetables, grains and beans. While any short noodle will work, my pasta of choice is whole-wheat or regular orzo. This recipe makes six hearty, filling bowls with only 300 calories per serving.

1 tbsp (15 ml) extra virgin olive oil

1 small white onion, finely diced

1½ cups (190 g) carrots, diced

1 cup (225 g) celery, diced

3 cloves garlic, peeled and minced

6 cups (1.4 L) vegetable broth

1 (14-oz [400-g]) can fire-roasted diced tomatoes

8 oz (225 g) whole-wheat small pasta such as orzo, ditalini, pastina, mini farfalle or mini penne

1 (15-oz [425-g]) can cannellini beans, drained and rinsed

½ tsp dried thyme

½ tsp dried oregano

¼ tsp dried rosemary

4 cups (120 g) loosely packed spinach leaves

Salt and freshly ground black pepper

Crushed red pepper flakes to taste

Heat oil in a large saucepan over medium-high heat. Add onion, carrots, celery and garlic and sauté for 10 minutes, until vegetables are tender and onion is translucent. Add vegetable broth, tomatoes, pasta, beans, thyme, oregano and rosemary, and stir to combine.

Bring soup to a simmer, stirring occasionally. Reduce heat to medium-low and simmer until pasta is just al dente.

Stir in the spinach and cook for 2–3 minutes until it is bright green and wilted. Season with salt, pepper and crushed red pepper flakes to taste. Serve warm.

vegetables, antipasti, salads and go-withs

Dinner in my house typically comprises some variety of pasta followed by Grandma's Green Salad (page 160). I know it's commonplace to eat salad before the meal, but I grew up eating it after the main course, so that's become my preferred order. While I'm uncertain of its origin, my grandmother told us that the roughage of the salad helped digest the pasta that came before it. Even if that's an old wives' tale, salad is a delicious and refreshing way to end a meal.

These recipes showcase how vegetables are meant to be prepared, with minimal fuss and maximum flavor. I recommend eating as close to in season as possible, knowing that a tomato in July will taste much different than a tomato in January. Eating in season makes cooking much easier. You don't have to fuss with additional flavors if Mother Nature gets it right first.

ROASTED BEET AND MOZZARELLA SALAD

— SERVES 4 —

This gorgeous salad is all about the layers of flavor: roasted beets, creamy avocado and fresh mozzarella.
It's a marriage of tender, earthy beets with the bright flavors of summer.
For a beautiful side dish, use a mix of both red and yellow beets.

6–8 medium beets, red, yellow or a mix of both

1 tsp extra virgin olive oil

Salt

DRESSING

1 shallot, finely chopped

⅓ cup (79 ml) extra virgin olive oil

2 tbsp (30 ml) white balsamic vinegar

Salt and freshly ground black pepper

½ cup (60 g) ciliegine (mozzarella balls), halved

1 large, ripe avocado, pit removed, cubed

2 cups (40 g) arugula

3 tbsp (10 g) pistachios, chopped

Preheat oven to 400°F (204°C).

Wash and trim the beets and pat dry. Place the beets on a piece of foil, enough to wrap around 2–4 beets, making 2–3 foil packets. Drizzle with 1 teaspoon olive oil and a pinch of salt. Wrap the beets tightly and place on a baking sheet. Bake for 50–90 minutes until tender, depending on the size of the beets. Remove from the oven, unwrap and set aside to cool.

Once cooled, peel the skin off the beets and slice into large chunks. Place in a bowl.

To make the dressing, place the finely chopped shallot in a bowl and whisk in the olive oil, balsamic vinegar and a pinch each of salt and pepper. Whisk until thick and emulsified, and set aside.

Place the ciliegine and avocado in the bowl with the beets along with ⅔ of the prepared dressing. Gently toss and let sit for 5 minutes to marinate.

Add the arugula to the bowl and toss once more to combine. Divide salad among 4 plates and garnish with pistachios. Drizzle with remaining dressing.

PARMESAN ASPARAGUS

— SERVES 4 AS A SIDE DISH —

**In this perfect side dish, tender, fresh asparagus is roasted to perfection
and topped with salty Parmesan and fresh lemon juice.**

1 bunch asparagus, woody ends removed

1 tbsp (15 ml) extra virgin olive oil

Salt and freshly ground black pepper

1 tbsp (15 ml) fresh lemon juice

3 tbsp (35 g) Parmesan cheese, freshly grated

Preheat the oven to 400°F (204°C).

Toss the asparagus with oil and pinch each of salt and pepper. Place in a single layer on a baking sheet and roast for 12–15 minutes until asparagus is tender and ends are slightly crispy.

Remove from oven and transfer to a platter. Drizzle with lemon juice and sprinkle on Parmesan cheese.

VEGAN VERSION: Replace Parmesan cheese with Vegan Parmesan Cheese (page 182), same amount.

GARLICKY BROCCOLI RABE

– SERVES 4 AS A SIDE DISH –

This is one of my favorite side dishes and something I make all the time. While broccoli rabe is my favorite here, any vegetable will work. Try this easy dish with broccolini, broccoli or thin green beans.

16 oz (455 g [about 1 bunch]) broccoli rabe, non-leafy stems removed

1 tbsp (15 ml) extra virgin olive oil

3 large cloves garlic, minced

¼ tsp crushed red pepper flakes

Salt and freshly ground black pepper

Bring a large pot of salted water to a boil. While the water is boiling, prepare a large bowl of ice water and place next to the stove.

Place the broccoli rabe in the boiling water and cook for 90 seconds, until bright green in color. Remove from the hot water and immediately place in the ice bowl to cool.

While the broccoli rabe is cooling, heat the olive oil in a large skillet over medium heat. Add the garlic and crushed red pepper flakes and cook for 30 seconds–1 minute until the pepper is fragrant and the garlic is lightly browned. Add in the cooked broccoli rabe from the water bath and toss a few times to combine and season. Season with a pinch each of salt and pepper.

LENTIL AND ROASTED RED PEPPER SALAD

— SERVES 4–6 AS A SIDE DISH —

This colorful salad combines smoky roasted peppers with salty feta, bright lemon juice and tender lentils.
It's one of my favorite salads, and I often make it on Sunday to snack on throughout the week. Eat it by
itself, as a side dish or stuffed into pita bread for a light, Mediterranean-inspired lunch.

2 large red bell peppers

1 cup (190 g) green lentils

½ medium red onion

1 stalk celery, halved

1 bay leaf

1 tsp dried thyme

2 tbsp (30 ml) red wine vinegar

2 tbsp (30 ml) extra virgin olive oil

1 tbsp (15 ml) fresh lemon juice

1 tsp Dijon mustard

2 cloves garlic, minced

½ tsp salt

½ tsp freshly ground black pepper

1 tbsp (2.5 g) fresh parsley leaves,
chopped

¼ cup (35 g) ricotta salata, crumbled
(can substitute feta cheese or crumbled
goat cheese, or omit completely)

Preheat the broiler to high and place the rack under the broiler about 4 inches
(10 cm) from the heat source. Wash the peppers and place on a foil-lined baking
sheet. Broil, turning the peppers as each side starts to blister and brown, until they
have collapsed. This should take anywhere from 15–30 minutes depending on the
size of your peppers.

While the peppers are broiling, make the lentils. Place lentils, onion, celery, bay leaf
and thyme in a saucepan and cover with water. Bring to a boil, reduce heat to low
and simmer, uncovered, until lentils are tender, about 20 minutes. Drain and place
lentils in a serving bowl, discarding the onion, celery and bay leaf.

Remove the sheet from the oven and very carefully slide the peppers into a bowl
and cover with a kitchen towel to let steam, about 10 minutes. Remove the towel
and let peppers cool until you can handle them, about 15 more minutes. Remove the
blistered skins, seeds and stems and thinly slice into strips.

Whisk together vinegar, oil, lemon juice, mustard, garlic, salt and pepper in a small
bowl. Add to the lentils and toss well. Stir into the lentils along with bell pepper,
parsley and ricotta salata.

*See photo on page 146.

VEGAN VERSION: Omit the ricotta salata.

BAKED SUMMER SQUASH GRATIN

— SERVES 6–8 AS A SIDE DISH —

Gratin, a simple casserole with a crisp golden crust, is another cherished side dish. Paired with a simple salad, it's a comforting and healthy meal that I turn to over and over again. While all produce works, this squash and zucchini version is my favorite. Gratin is typically made with heavy cream and lots of cheese. I've lightened up with a version that focuses on only the essentials: creamy zucchini filling with a crispy Parmesan crust. It's the same familiar flavor of your favorite gratin, with less than half of the calories and fat.

4 cups (515 g) yellow squash, sliced

4 cups (450 g) zucchini, sliced

3 tbsp (45 g) butter

½ cup (50 g) Parmesan cheese, freshly grated

½ cup (55 g) bread crumbs

Salt and freshly ground black pepper

1 tsp dried parsley

1 tsp garlic powder

¾ cup (180 ml) low-fat milk

Preheat the oven to 400°F (204°C).

Layer alternating slices of squash and zucchini in a baking pan or gratin dish. Lightly dot with 1 tablespoon (15 g) of butter, trying to spread out the butter as much as possible over the layer. Continue with another layer of squash/zucchini, 1 tablespoon (15 g) of butter, and a final layer of squash/zucchini and butter. In total, you should have three layers of squash alternating with butter.

Mix together the Parmesan, bread crumbs, a pinch each of salt and pepper, parsley and garlic powder. Pour milk over the layered zucchini and sprinkle bread crumb mixture on in an even layer.

Bake for 25–30 minutes or until bubbly and browned.

SIMPLE BROCCOLI SALAD

— SERVES 4-6 AS A SIDE DISH —

I once made this dish for a friend's bridal shower and years later, I still get asked for the recipe. Be prepared, this has serious garlic flavor. To prevent anyone from biting into a hunk of raw garlic, finely mince the garlic clove using a knife or microplane and then press into a thin paste.

1 head broccoli

DRESSING

3 cloves garlic, minced

3 tbsp extra virgin olive oil

Salt and freshly ground black pepper

Trim the woody end off the broccoli and peel the outer stem. Slice the florets into thin stems, keeping the floret and stalk part attached.

Finely mince the garlic cloves and use the side of a large knife to press the minced garlic into a cutting board. Continue to go back and forth along the minced garlic until a paste is formed. Place the paste in a small bowl and whisk in the olive oil and a pinch each of salt and pepper.

Bring a large pot of salted water to a boil. Add the broccoli to the salted water and cook until bright green and tender when pierced with a fork, about 3 minutes.

Remove the broccoli and place in a large bowl. Add the dressing and toss to combine. Serve at room temperature.

CHICKPEA SALAD

— SERVES 4 AS A SIDE DISH —

I've been eating this salad since I was a little girl. It's one of my mom's favorite quick salads, and I often make it into a meal along with a few ears of grilled corn and tomato and basil salad. To tame the bite of raw red onions, I quickly pickle them in red wine vinegar while I am preparing the rest of the ingredients. After soaking, drain and toss with the salad. You'll get all the flavor from the onion, without any unpleasant side effects.

½ cup (60 g) red onion, finely chopped

2 tbsp (30 ml) red wine vinegar

1 (15-oz [425-g]) can chickpeas, rinsed and drained

2 tbsp (30 ml) fresh lemon juice

1 tbsp (15 ml) extra virgin olive oil

½ cup (15 g) fresh parsley leaves, chopped

1 tbsp (10 g) capers, rinsed and coarsely chopped

Salt and freshly ground black pepper, to taste

Place the red onion and red wine vinegar in a bowl and stir to combine. Let sit while you prepare the rest of the salad. The red wine will cut some of the harshness of the raw onion, making it more palatable.

Toss together the chickpeas, lemon juice, olive oil, parsley and capers. Season with a generous pinch each of salt and pepper and let sit for 10 minutes to marinate.

Drain the onion and toss with the chickpea salad. Season with salt and pepper to taste, if needed, and serve.

ARUGULA AND PARMESAN SALAD

— SERVES 4 AS A SIDE DISH —

I serve this simple salad at least once a week. It's ready in about two minutes flat and only requires chopping the parsley. I buy a few bags of arugula at a time, as I love its peppery bite; it's delicious in salads, sandwiches and smoothies.

1 (7-oz [200-g]) bag arugula leaves

⅛ cup (5 g) fresh parsley leaves, roughly chopped

DRESSING

1 tbsp (15 ml) fresh lemon juice

2 tbsp (30 ml) extra olive oil

2 tsp (10 ml) balsamic vinegar

⅛ tsp crushed red pepper flakes

½ tsp flaked sea salt, plus more to taste

¼ tsp freshly ground black pepper, plus more to taste

¼ cup (24 g) shaved Parmesan cheese

Toss arugula and parsley together in a large salad bowl.

Whisk together lemon juice, olive oil, balsamic vinegar, crushed red pepper flakes, salt and pepper. Drizzle onto the arugula mixture and toss well. Add in Parmesan and toss once more to serve. Season to taste, if needed, with salt and pepper.

ZUCCHINI CAPRESE SALAD

— SERVES 4 AS A SIDE DISH —

This beautiful, fresh summer salad is my vegan take on caprese salad. The avocado adds creaminess and easily replaces the mozzarella. This salad should almost melt in your mouth, so take care to slice the zucchini as papery-thin as possible. Ribbons of zucchini, avocado and fresh basil—who needs the cheese?

2 medium zucchini

1 pint (300 g) cherry tomatoes, halved

1 tbsp (15 ml) fresh lemon juice

3 tbsp (45 ml) balsamic vinegar

2 tbsp (30 ml) extra virgin olive oil

1 medium clove garlic, minced

Salt and freshly ground black pepper

1 ripe Haas avocado, cut into cubes

½ cup (10 g) fresh basil, thinly sliced

If the zucchini is large, cut in half lengthwise, then very thinly slice using a knife or a mandoline. A mandoline produces even, thin slices. If zucchini is medium or small, no need to cut in half first, just thinly slice. Place the zucchini and tomatoes in a large bowl.

In a small bowl, whisk together the lemon juice, vinegar, olive oil, garlic, salt and pepper.

Add to the zucchini bowl, toss together and let sit for 10 minutes to marinate.

Add in the avocado and basil. Lightly toss to combine and serve immediately.

GRANDMA'S GREEN SALAD

— SERVES 4-6 —

Growing up, we ate salad every single night, typically some version of the recipe below. Lettuce was always included, as was whatever vegetables my mom had on hand. One thing that never wavered was the dressing, a simple drizzle of quality extra virgin olive oil, red wine vinegar and plenty of salt and pepper. I know the salt seems like a lot, but it totally makes the dish. Once you try this simple dressing, you may never go back to store-bought vinaigrette again.

2 heads romaine lettuce

1 large tomato, chopped

1 carrot, chopped

2 scallions, chopped

2 tbsp (30 ml) extra virgin olive oil

1 tbsp (15 ml) red wine vinegar

1 tsp salt, divided

Freshly ground black pepper

Wash the lettuce and thoroughly dry. Tear or chop into bite-sized pieces and place into a large bowl. Add the tomato, carrot and scallions and lightly toss together.

Drizzle on the oil, vinegar, ¾ teaspoon salt and a generous sprinkle of pepper. Toss together and season to taste, adding remaining ¼ teaspoon salt if desired. Enjoy immediately.

homemade pasta

Making homemade pasta is meditation for me. I zone out while I roll out sheets of fresh pasta or cut individual squares of ravioli. If you've never made homemade pasta before, I urge you to give it a try. While it may take a little bit of practice to work the dough, once you get the hang of it, it only gets easier. Using a pasta machine or stand mixer attachment significantly cuts down on the work, making homemade pasta a semi-regular treat. If you don't have the equipment, put it on your wish list and enjoy the Homemade Gnocchi (page 172), Homemade Manicotti (page 165) and wonton raviolis (Fresh Ricotta and Spinach Ravioli [page 169] and Butternut Squash Ravioli with Spinach Pesto [page 177]), none of which rely on a pasta machine.

My husband Bryan and I have turned homemade-pasta-making into our date-night in. We'll open a bottle of wine, start the sauce and then spend quality time together in the kitchen rolling and cutting. It's a great way to relax and connect while we create a satisfying meal that's better (and less expensive) than what we could find at a restaurant.

HOMEMADE MANICOTTI

— MAKES ABOUT 10 MANICOTTI, CAN EASILY BE DOUBLED OR TRIPLED —

This recipe is what I know to be manicotti: fluffy crepes filled with a creamy ricotta, then covered in homemade red sauce. While it's traditionally served for both Christmas and Easter, it makes a regular appearance in my house for dinner parties and evenings where only homemade pasta will do. Over the years, I've tried adding various vegetables to the filling, but prefer this simple version best. To add in more nutrients, I typically serve alongside a gorgeous green salad or my Simple Broccoli Salad (page 154) To make ahead of time, prepare the manicotti but do not bake. Cover tightly with plastic or foil, freeze, then bake directly from frozen.

CREPE BATTER

1 cup (125 g) all-purpose flour

1 cup (240 ml) water

¼ tsp salt

4 eggs

1 tsp extra virgin olive oil or cooking spray, for pan

FILLING

8 oz (225 g) part-skim ricotta

1 tbsp (10 g) sugar

1 large egg

Cinnamon

Nutmeg, freshly ground

3–4 cups (720–960 ml) marinara sauce or Sunday Red Sauce (page 181)

In a large bowl, place the flour, water and salt and mix until smooth; add eggs one at a time until fully incorporated and well blended.

Heat a crepe pan or small nonstick skillet over medium heat. Lightly spray with cooking spray or swirl in 1 teaspoon of olive oil, just enough to coat the bottom of the pan.

Add a small amount of batter to the warm skillet and tilt until the bottom of the skillet is covered in batter. Let sit until firm, but not brown, about 30 seconds–1 minute. Flip and cook on the other side. Remove from skillet and place on a large plate or cutting board. Repeat until batter is gone, placing pieces of wax paper between crepes so they don't stick to each other.

In a separate bowl, whisk together the ricotta, sugar, egg and a small pinch each of cinnamon and nutmeg.

Preheat the oven to 350°F (176°C).

Spread a thin layer of red sauce in the bottom of a 9x13-inch (23x33-cm) glass pan. Dollop a small amount of filling onto a prepared crepe and roll up. Place seam-side down into the glass pan and repeat with remaining crepes. Cover with sauce and bake for 35–40 minutes.

SWEET POTATO GNOCCHI WITH BALSAMIC BROWN BUTTER AND SAGE SAUCE

— SERVES 4–6 —

I love the process of making of homemade gnocchi. It's the perfect excuse to pour myself a glass of wine, put on some music and spend a few hours in the kitchen. Since it's a laborious process to make homemade pasta, I'm including a fairly large recipe, enough for about 150 gnocchi. I'd rather make once, cook twice, so I recommend making the entire gnocchi recipe and then freezing whatever you don't use. Cooked gnocchi doesn't keep very well, so only cook off what you think you will need.

With homemade pasta, I like to keep the sauces simple so the beauty of the noodle shines through. This Balsamic Brown Butter and Sage Sauce is a heavenly addition to sweet potato gnocchi, but any sauce will do.

GNOCCHI

1½ lb (680 g) sweet potatoes

½ lb (225 g) russet potatoes

1 tsp salt

½ tsp freshly ground black pepper

¼ cup (25 g) Parmesan cheese, freshly grated

1 large egg, lightly beaten

1½–2 cups (188–250 g) all-purpose wheat flour

BROWN BUTTER AND SAGE SAUCE

4 tbsp (55 g) unsalted butter

7–8 fresh sage leaves

2 tbsp (30 ml) balsamic vinegar

½ tsp salt

¼ tsp freshly ground black pepper

¼ tsp crushed red pepper flakes

½ cup (60 g) walnuts, toasted and finely chopped

Scrub clean all the potatoes, then poke with a fork several times to allow space for steam to escape.

Preheat oven to 425°F (218°C) and arrange a rack in the middle. Place potatoes on a rimmed baking sheet and roast for 45–50 minutes until fork tender. As an alternative, you can microwave potatoes for 5–7 minutes until tender.

Remove from oven and set aside until just cool enough to handle. Remove the skin and scoop out the flesh. Press potato flesh through a potato ricer or lightly mash with back of a fork and place in a large bowl. Stir in the salt, pepper, Parmesan cheese and lightly beaten egg.

Add the flour ½ cup (60 g) at a time until soft dough forms. Depending on the moisture of the potatoes, you may not need all the flour. You want the dough to be damp, but not sticky. The more flour you add, the denser the dough will be, so start easy and then add more if needed. The goal is to add as little as flour as necessary to create a soft, cohesive dough. Let rest for 10 minutes on the counter.

Gently pat dough into a large square and divide into 12 equal pieces. I divide by 6 lengthwise, then 6 widthwise.

Generously flour a cutting board and roll out each piece of dough into a long rope, roughly ½ inch (1.3 cm) in diameter. If the dough is sticky, lightly sprinkle with additional flour.

Cut each rope into ½-inch (1.3-cm) pieces. You can stop here and keep the gnocchi in little dumplings, which I think look beautiful for sweet potato gnocchi, or create little pockets.

To create little pockets with your fingers, use your pointer and middle fingers to pull the lower ½ of the gnocchi piece toward you, and then flip the top over to create a crevice in the center. You can also roll each gnocchi piece over the tines of a fork to create grooves.

(continued)

Bring a large pot of salted water to a boil; reduce heat to a gentle simmer and add the gnocchi, in batches, until tender. Once they are tender and float to the top of the pot, remove with a slotted spoon and transfer to a rimmed baking sheet. You want to keep them in a single layer while the rest of the gnocchi are cooking so they don't stick to one another.

While the water is boiling, make the sauce. Melt the butter in a medium saucepan over medium heat, stirring occasionally. Cook the butter until the foam dissipates and the butter begins to turn a golden-brown color, about 4 minutes. Reduce heat to low and add in the sage leaves, allowing them to crisp for 1 minute. Remove with a slotted spoon and finely chop or crumble.

Remove sauce from heat and stir in the vinegar, salt, pepper and crushed red pepper flakes. Season to taste and toss with gnocchi and toasted walnuts.

NOTE: If making ahead, gnocchi can be made up to this point and then frozen. To freeze, place gnocchi in a single layer on a baking sheet in the freezer until completely frozen. Transfer to an airtight container and keep frozen for up to 2 months. Cook from frozen.

FRESH RICOTTA AND SPINACH RAVIOLI

— SERVES 4 —

Wonton wrappers, found in the refrigerated section of most grocery stores near the tofu, are a good substitute for fresh pasta when making homemade ravioli. The dough is light and thin, a quick and easy shortcut for when you want homemade ravioli on a weeknight.

FILLING

1 cup (30 g) fresh, cooked or frozen spinach, squeezed, finely chopped

¼ cup (30 g) mozzarella, grated

¾ cup (185 g) low-fat ricotta

⅛ cup (15 g) Parmesan cheese, freshly grated

¼ tsp nutmeg, freshly ground

Salt and freshly ground black pepper, to taste

24 square wonton wrappers

3 cups (700 ml) marinara sauce or Sunday Red Sauce (page 181)

Fresh basil, chopped, to garnish

Parmesan cheese, to garnish

In a large bowl combine the spinach, mozzarella, ricotta, Parmesan cheese and nutmeg, and salt and pepper to taste.

Work with 1–2 wonton skins at a time, keeping the others covered with plastic wrap. Lightly moisten the edge of the wrapper with water.

Place a heaping teaspoon of filling in the center of each wrap and fold two ends together, forming a triangle. Gently press out the air and crimp the edges tightly with a fork or your fingers to seal. Once they are filled, transfer the ravioli to a flour-dusted sheet pan and spread in a single layer. Repeat with the remaining wonton wrappers and filling.

Bring a large pot of water to a boil and add ravioli. Reduce heat to medium low and cook, until just tender, about 2–3 minutes.

While the water is boiling, heat the sauce in a medium saucepan.

To serve, remove ravioli with a slotted spoon (to reduce excess water) and divide among 4 plates. Cover with sauce. Garnish with basil and Parmesan cheese.

HOMEMADE PASTA

— MAKES 1½ POUNDS (680 G) —

My husband loves homemade pasta so much, he referenced it in our wedding vows. We often joke that he proposed soon after tasting my homemade pasta with Wild Mushroom Ragù (page 91). I'd like to think he proposed because of my killer sense of humor, but I digress. If I had to choose only one homemade pasta recipe I'd want everyone to attempt to make, it's this one. I've included directions for making pasta using a machine, but you can create pasta sheets using a rolling pin. Just be prepared to get a really great workout in the process. The sheets should be almost thin enough to see your fingers through the dough. Any thinner and they will tear when cut; too thick, they will be dense and chewy.

3 cups (375 g) all-purpose flour

4 large eggs

1 tsp salt

Mound the flour in the center of a large wooden board or cutting board, or for less mess, you can do this method in a large bowl. Make a shallow well in the center of the flour and add in the eggs and salt. Using a fork, beat the eggs and then begin to push in some of the flour, starting with the inner rim of the well. As you mix in the flour, keep pushing the flour up to retain the well shape.

When roughly half of the flour is added, the dough will begin to come together. Knead together until uniform in texture, about 5 minutes, adding extra flour as necessary. The dough should be elastic and a little sticky. Wrap the dough in plastic wrap and allow to rest for 30 minutes at room temperature before using.

Set your pasta machine to the thickest setting. Roughly flatten one piece of dough between your hands like a patty and feed it through the pasta roller. Repeat. Fold this piece of dough into thirds, like folding a letter, and flatten it between your hands again. Feed it through once or twice more until smooth.

This next step is optional, but it helps to develop the gluten, creating a more delicate pasta noodle.

Once the pasta is flattened, change the settings on your roller to roll the pasta thinner and thinner. Roll the pasta two or three times at each setting. Don't be tempted to skip a setting as the pasta may break if you do. If the pasta sheet becomes too long, slice it in half.

Cut the dough into noodle-length sheets, about 12 inches (30.5 cm). Switch from the pasta roller to the noodle cutter and run the sheet through the noodle cutter. Toss the noodles with a little bit of flour and set aside. Continue with the rest of the noodles. I find it easiest to roll the pasta all at once before cutting it into noodles.

To cook the pasta immediately, bring a large pot of water to a boil and cook the pasta until al dente, about 4–5 minutes. Serve with pasta sauce of choice.

To dry, lay the pasta on a drying rack, coat hangers or the back of a chair, and let air dry until completely brittle. Store in an airtight container for several weeks.

To freeze, either freeze flat in long noodles or in a bird's nest shape. Place in an airtight container and freeze for up to 3 months. Cook directly from frozen, adding an extra 1–2 minutes to the cooking time.

HOMEMADE GNOCCHI

– SERVES 4 –

Some of my favorite memories of my grandmother's kitchen involve making homemade gnocchi, my small, child's hands trying so hard to roll the potato dumplings as effortlessly as my grandmother. I know there are several tools available for rolling gnocchi, but I'm including the technique that was passed down to me. Once you've cut the gnocchi, use your pointer and middle fingers to pull the bottom half of the gnocchi toward you, then roll the remaining half on top, creating a crevice for sauce to nestle into. I have a video on my website, delishknowledge.com, showing the technique in more detail.

I've shared this recipe with many people, and find that it usually takes one or two times to get the technique and figure out how the dough should look and feel. Don't be discouraged if it turns out slightly gummy the first time. It's easy to over-knead the dough. To cut down on the possibility of overworking the dough and create light, fluffy gnocchi, I highly suggest using a potato ricer.

2 large baking potatoes (about 2 lb [906 g] baking potatoes)

1 tsp salt

1¼ cups (155 g) all-purpose flour, divided

Preheat oven to 400°F (204°C). Clean the potatoes and poke all over with a fork. Bake for 1 hour until really soft. Remove from the oven and peel off the skins.

Using a ricer, rice potatoes and place in a large bowl. If you don't have a ricer, mash until there are as few lumps as possible. This works best when potatoes are still relatively warm, so try and remove the skins and mash as soon as you are able to handle the potatoes. The easiest way is to chop the potato into a fine dice and then gently use your fork to mash into a finer consistency. Take care not to over mash or the dough will become gummy. You want an even consistency without lumps. Let cool.

Once you've processed the potatoes, put them on a large cutting board and use a spoon to gently push the potatoes down into an even, thin layer on the surface. Take care not to smash or drag the potatoes as that will make them gummy. Just gently press down to remove as much moisture as possible.

Once the potatoes are in a pile, sprinkle with salt and ½ cup (65 g) flour. Using a large spatula, stab downward to cut the flour into the potato, while will absorb most of it. Fold ⅓ of the potato in from the side, then fold another ⅓ of the potato in from the other side and lightly press down. Sprinkle another ½ cup (65 g) of flour over the potato and stab downward again, cutting into the potato. By now, a dough will be starting to form. After you cut in a second time, gather the dough into a round with your hands, gently pressing together but not kneading it.

Sprinkle 1–2 tablespoons (10–15 g) of flour over the dough mound and gently knead the dough to just incorporate the flour. You want the dough to be moist, but not too sticky. If you need more flour, add it here. Depending on the moisture in your potatoes, you may need more or less. Start with less as you can always add more. Once the dough feels pliable but still a bit tacky, you're done. Pat the dough into a large, round disk, dust with a bit more flour and wrap in plastic wrap. Let dough rest for 30 minutes.

At this point, I usually make whatever sauce I am going to serve with my gnocchi. My Sunday Red Sauce (page 181) or Protein-Packed Pesto (page 189) are my favorite choices, but anything goes.

Unwrap dough and place onto a lightly flour-dusted workspace. Divide the dough into 8 sections and roll each section into a ½-inch (1.3-cm) thick log. Cut the rope into 1-inch (2.5-cm) pieces. Using your pointed and middle fingers, pull a piece of dough toward you. Fold the other side over. You want to make a crevice where sauce can get in.

Bring a large pot of salted water to a boil. Place gnocchi in water and cook until they rise to the surface, about 3 minutes. Do this in batches, being sure not to overcrowd the gnocchi in the pot. Have a large platter or bowl ready with a bit of whatever sauce or pesto you'll be serving on the gnocchi. Place the gnocchi on the platter. Continue cooking in batches until all the gnocchi are done. Gently toss with more sauce or pesto and serve immediately.

Only cook the amount of gnocchi you intend to use. Freeze any additional gnocchi before cooking. Boil straight from frozen for about 5 minutes, until they float to the top. To freeze, place in a single layer on a baking sheet and freeze until hard. Then place in a freezer-safe container for up to 6 months.

HOMEMADE RAVIOLI WITH MUSHROOM FILLING

— SERVES 6-8 —

When it comes to fresh pasta, the reward is worth the effort! Nothing compares to the delicate taste of fresh pasta, especially when stuffed with a rich mushroom filling. Like anything new, making this ravioli the first time may take a while but once you get the hang of it, you'll discover how easy homemade pasta can be. I like to double the recipe and freeze half. To do so, place prepared ravioli in a single layer on a baking sheet in the freezer until frozen. Then place frozen ravioli in a freezer bag or freezer-safe container. Cook from frozen in simmering, not boiling, water, until ravioli come to the top.

Make sure to cook the mushroom filling until very dry as it will thicken and make the pasta easier to stuff. Any variety of mushrooms work here. I've included my favorite combo of flavors. Taste and season your filling before stuffing—it should be good enough to eat on its own with a spoon!

MUSHROOM FILLING

10 oz (285 g) cremini mushrooms

5 oz (140 g) oyster mushrooms

2 tbsp (30 g) butter

2 shallots, finely diced

3 garlic cloves, minced

½ tsp dried thyme

Salt and freshly ground black pepper

½ cup (80 ml) red wine

½ cup (90 g) Parmesan cheese, freshly grated

RAVIOLI DOUGH

3 cups (375 g) all-purpose flour

½ tsp salt

4 large eggs

Make the filling. Using either a food processor or knife, finely chop the mushrooms into pieces no larger than ½ inch (1.3 cm). Heat the butter in a large skillet over medium heat and add mushrooms. Cook until softened, about 3-5 minutes. Add in the shallots, garlic, thyme and pinch each of salt and pepper. Reduce heat to low and continue to cook, stirring occasionally, until mixture is dry, about 15 minutes. Add the red wine and increase heat to medium high. Cook, stirring, until liquid is absorbed, about 5 minutes. Remove from heat and stir in the Parmesan cheese. Season to taste with salt and pepper.

Place filling into a food processor and puree until smooth. Set aside while you make the ravioli dough.

Mound the flour in the center of a large wooden board or cutting board. Make a shallow well in the center of the flour and add in the salt and eggs. Using a fork, beat the eggs and then begin to push in some of the flour; starting with the inner rim of the well. As you mix in the flour, keep pushing the flour up to retain the well shape.

For less mess, you can do this in a bowl, mix as directed and then knead on the counter.

When roughly half of the flour is added, the dough will begin to come together. Knead together until uniform in texture, about 10 minutes, adding extra flour as necessary. The dough should be elastic and a little sticky. If it's too dry, add 1-2 tablespoons (15-30 ml) of cold water. Wrap the dough in plastic wrap and allow to rest for 30 minutes at room temperature before using.

Sprinkle a cutting board generously with flour. Divide the dough into 8 equal portions. Dust the portions with flour and cover with a clean dish towel. You want to make sure that everything is well floured to prevent the pasta from sticking to itself and to the pasta machine. If the dough starts to feel sticky, sprinkle with more flour. Covering the dough that you aren't using prevents it from drying out and becoming brittle.

(continued)

Set your pasta machine to the thickest setting. Roughly flatten 1 of the 8 portions of dough between your hands into a patty and feed it through the pasta roller. Repeat. Fold this piece of dough into thirds, like folding a letter, and flatten it between your hands again. Feed it through once or twice more until smooth.

Once the pasta is flattened, change the settings on your roller to roll the pasta thinner and thinner. Roll the pasta 2 or 3 times at each settings. Don't be tempted to skip a setting as the pasta may break if you do. You want the pasta thin, but not too thin. I typically stop at the second-to-last setting. As you roll the pasta out thinner and thinner, it may become too long to handle. In this case, slice in half. Place finished pasta sheet on a floured surface and cover with a kitchen towel so the pasta doesn't dry out and become brittle. Continue with the rest of the dough portions until finished.

To fill, place one sheet of pasta on a floured cutting board and slice any excess off so that the pasta is a near-perfect rectangle. Place heaping tablespoons along the lower half of the dough, keeping ½ inch (1.3 cm) of space between the fillings.

Using a pastry brush, moisten the edge of the lower half of dough lightly with water. Fold the dough over along the crease, carefully pressing from the fold outward to remove excess air. Gently pat the dough down around each lump of filling to create a seal.

Cut each ravioli piece using the fluted side of a ravioli cutter. Continue with the rest of the pasta, covering the finished pieces with a kitchen towel.

To cook, bring a large pot of water to a boil, then reduce heat to a simmer. Make sure water is simmering, not boiling. If water is boiling, ravioli may fall apart. Cook for 3 minutes, until dough is cooked through. It should rise to the top of the pot once finished.

Remove with a slotted spoon and serve with sauce of choice. These ravioli are so delicate, I usually just serve with a generous drizzle of extra virgin olive oil and more fresh Parmesan cheese.

BUTTERNUT SQUASH RAVIOLI WITH SPINACH PESTO

— SERVES 4–6 —

These vegan butternut squash ravioli are a great way to highlight the flavors of fall without a lot of excess fat and cholesterol. As a shortcut, I'm relying on fresh, eggless wonton wrappers, but if you're up for it, enjoy this ravioli with my homemade ravioli dough (page 174). Not all wonton wrappers are vegan, but most Asian grocery stores carry eggless wrappers.

While toasting the walnuts is optional, it's a simple trick that really brings out the buttery flavor and texture of fresh walnuts. Heat nuts in a dry, heavy skillet over medium heat for 1 to 2 minutes or until they're golden brown and they give off a rich, toasty fragrance. Watch them closely so they don't burn.

FILLING

1 medium butternut squash, halved lengthwise and seeded

1 tsp dried oregano

1 tbsp (15 ml) olive oil

1 tbsp (5 g) nutritional yeast

¼ tsp nutmeg, freshly ground

Salt and freshly ground black pepper

32 eggless/vegan wonton wrappers

SPINACH PESTO

2 garlic cloves

1½ cups (45 g) fresh spinach leaves

½ cup (45 g) fresh basil leaves

⅓ cup (40 g) toasted walnuts halves

1 tbsp (5 g) nutritional yeast

2 tbsp (30 ml) olive oil

2 tbsp (30 ml) vegetable broth

1 tbsp (15 ml) fresh lemon juice

Preheat the oven to 400°F (204°C).

Place the squash halves cut-side down on a foil or parchment-paper-lined baking sheet. Bake for 30–40 minutes, until fork tender. Remove from oven and let cool until able to handle. Scoop out the flesh. You should have about 2 cups (330 g) pulp from the squash.

Place the butternut pulp in a large bowl and gently mash with the oregano, olive oil, nutritional yeast, nutmeg and a large pinch each of salt and pepper. Season to taste, as needed.

Prepare a small bowl of water and set near your working area. Working with 1 wonton wrapper at a time, spoon about 1 teaspoon squash mixture into the center of each wrapper. Moisten the edges of the wrapper and fold the wrapper in half to form a triangle. Pinch edges together with a fork or your fingers to form a seal. Repeat procedure with remaining wrappers and place on a lightly floured baking sheet.

Make the pesto. Place the garlic, spinach, basil, walnut halves and nutritional yeast in the base of a food processor and pulse until finely chopped. With the motor running, slowly pour in the oil, broth and lemon juice. Process until very well blended. Place in a large bowl.

Bring a large pot of salted water to a boil. Add half of the ravioli (or less depending on the size of your pot) and cook for 2–3 minutes, until ravioli is cooked through. Gently remove ravioli with a slotted spoon and place in the pesto bowl. Cook the remaining ravioli and gently toss with pesto to coat. Serve immediately.

the basics

These recipes are quick and easy staples that I make at home as often as possible. While jarred sauces are everywhere, they don't compare to my Sunday Red Sauce (page 181). It's easy to make a large batch of sauce once a month and freeze off the jars that you don't need for the week. For fast meals, I'm including two tomato sauce recipes that are ready in just 15 minutes.

I'm including my vegan versions of ricotta, heavy cream and Parmesan, so that most of these recipes can transform from vegetarian to vegan with a few simple swaps. Even if you're not vegan, these staples are so yummy and close to the real deal that I hope you'll be inspired to try them!

SUNDAY RED SAUCE

— MAKES ABOUT 7 CUPS (1.7 L) —

This is the first recipe I ever learned how to make and I've made it so often, I could probably do it in my sleep. My mom made this sauce at least two times a week when I was growing up, and paired with everything from spaghetti with meatballs to homemade manicotti and baked lasagna. While I do use jar sauce from time to time, I almost always have a few jars of this sauce tucked away in my freezer. It's a little more time consuming than my quick ragù, but the flavor can't be beat. It also doubles and triples beautifully so feel free to share extras with loved ones or store in freezer-safe containers for later.

The quality of tomatoes really matters here, so buy the best canned tomatoes you can find.
I swear by Hunt's, Muir Glen and San Marzano.

1 tbsp (15 ml) extra virgin olive oil

1 medium white or yellow onion, diced

1 green bell pepper, diced

1 tsp dried oregano

¼ tsp crushed red pepper flakes

3 cloves garlic, minced

¼ cup (60 ml) red wine (optional, for deglazing the vegetables)

2 tbsp (35 g) tomato paste

1 (29-oz [820-g]) can tomato sauce

1 (29-oz [820-g]) can crushed tomatoes

Salt and freshly ground black pepper

In a large stock pan, heat the olive oil over medium heat. Add the onion and green bell pepper and cook until onion is translucent and green bell pepper is tender, about 8–10 minutes. Add in the dried oregano, crushed red pepper flakes and garlic and cook for another 1–2 minutes until spices are fragrant and garlic has almost melted into the onion/pepper mixture.

Add the red wine and use a wooden spoon to gently scrape up any browned bits of onion. Whisk in the tomato paste and let simmer for 5–10 minutes until thick.

Add in the tomato sauce, crushed tomatoes and pinch each of salt and pepper and reduce heat to low. Cover, stirring occasionally, for at least 30 minutes. Season to taste and serve with anything!

VEGAN PARMESAN CHEESE

– MAKES ABOUT 1 CUP (100 G) –

I keep a shaker of this Vegan Parmesan Cheese in the fridge for anytime I need a yummy topping without the dairy. The salty, cheesy taste is the perfect substitute for cheese. You can find nutritional yeast in most well-stocked grocery stores or online. I like a mix of cashews and almonds, but feel free to use ¾ cup (85 g cashews, 130 g almonds) of either variety. Leftovers can be frozen up to 6 months.

¼ cup (34 g) raw cashews

½ cup (48 g) blanched almonds

¼ cup (48 g) nutritional yeast

½ tsp salt

1 tbsp (10 g) garlic powder

Combine all ingredients in a high-powered blender or food processor and pulse until a fine meal forms.

QUICK MARINARA

– MAKES ABOUT 3½ CUPS (828 ML) –

I rely on this quick marinara when I don't have time to make my Sunday Red Sauce (page 181). It's ready in about 15 minutes and only requires a handful of ingredients. For a spicier sauce, add in ⅛–¼ teaspoon crushed red pepper flakes. If you have fresh basil lying around, throw in a handful of chopped leaves at the end for a fresh flavor. Once it's made, the possibilities are endless! Serve with hot pasta, on toasted subs with veggie meatballs or as a base for lasagna and stuffed shells.

1 tbsp (15 ml) extra virgin olive oil

3 cloves garlic, minced

1 tsp Italian seasoning

½ tsp salt

½ tsp sugar

1 (29-oz [820-g]) can crushed tomatoes

Heat the olive oil in a medium saucepan over medium heat and add the garlic, Italian seasoning and salt. Cook, stirring often, for 30 seconds–1 minute until aromatic. Add in the sugar and crushed tomatoes and reduce heat to a low simmer. Cook, slightly covered, for 15–20 minutes.

CASHEW CREAM

— MAKES APPROXIMATELY 2 CUPS (360 ML) —

I'll never forget the first time I was introduced to the idea of cashew cream. How could something so luxurious come out of a jar of soaked cashews? I use this cashew cream in most recipes that call for heavy cream. A little bit goes a long way and it's the perfect healthy swap for cream. Think of this recipe as a launching point. From here you can go either sweet or savory with minimal effort. Try roasted garlic for a savory pasta sauce or a little maple syrup for a sweet, creamy topping.

The key to silky cashew cream is soaking the raw cashews for at least 1 hour, preferably longer. The longer they soak, the easier they will be to puree. If I'm in a hurry, I will place cashews in a bowl and then pour hot water over them for a quick 10-minute soak before using.

1½ cups (205 g) raw, unsalted cashews

¾ cup (180 ml) water, plus more for soaking

½–1 tsp salt

Place the cashews in a bowl and fill with enough water to cover at least 1 inch (2.5 cm) above the cashews. Allow the cashews to soak for 1 hour or up to overnight. Drain and rinse the cashews.

Place the cashews, water and salt in a high-powered blender or food processor. I usually start off with ½ teaspoon of salt and will add more if needed. If I am adding to a dish with other salt components, I will keep it on the less-salty side. Blend until creamy, silky and smooth, about 1–5 minutes depending on the power of your blender. It should be the consistency of cream when you are done. It should not be grainy.

Use as is or store in the refrigerator for 3–4 days. It can also be frozen for up to 6 months, then defrosted before using. If storing in the freezer, run it through the blender again after defrosting to make it uniform in texture.

CAULIFLOWER BÉCHAMEL

— MAKES ABOUT 5 CUPS (1.2 L) —

This creamy sauce is my lighter take on traditional béchamel sauce. I use it in my Wild Mushroom Lasagna (page 75), and it's delicious anywhere you need a cream sauce. For baked mac and cheese, stir shredded cheese of choice into this sauce, add pasta and bake until hot and bubbly.

5 cups (540 g) cauliflower florets (from one head of cauliflower)

4 tbsp (60 g) butter

¼ cup (45 g) all-purpose flour

4 cups (950 ml) skim or low-fat milk

⅛ tsp nutmeg, freshly ground

¼ cup (30 g) Parmesan cheese, freshly grated

Salt and freshly ground black pepper

Place cauliflower florets in a large microwave-safe bowl with enough water to just cover the bottom of the bowl. Cover bowl loosely with a paper towel and steam cauliflower in microwave on high until tender, 4–5 minutes; drain. Alternatively, you can bring a pot of water to a boil and place cauliflower in a steam basket and cook until fork tender, about 4–5 minutes.

Melt the butter in a saucepan over medium heat. Whisk in the flour and cook for 1 minute until golden brown. Gently whisk in the milk and increase the heat to medium high and bring to a boil. Continue to whisk, cooking until thick, about 5 minutes. Add in the cauliflower, reduce heat to low and simmer for another 5 minutes.

Remove from heat and let cool slightly. Transfer to a high-powered blender or food processor and puree until very smooth. Alternatively, use an immersion blender to puree. Add in the nutmeg, Parmesan cheese and a pinch each of salt and pepper and pulse a few times to combine. It should be the consistency of marinara sauce. If it's too thick, thin with more milk.

TOFU RICOTTA

— MAKES ABOUT 3 CUPS (370 G) —

Tofu is a wonderful replacement for ricotta cheese! Use this recipe anywhere you would use dairy ricotta— it's wonderful in lasagna, rollatini and stuffed shells.

2 tsp (10 ml) extra virgin olive oil

1 cup white or yellow onion, finely chopped

3 cloves garlic, minced

1 (14-oz [410-g]) package firm tofu, drained

1½ tsp (7.5 g) salt, plus more to taste

1 tsp freshly ground black pepper, plus more to taste

2 tbsp (30 ml) fresh lemon juice

3 cups (70 g) fresh basil

Heat the olive oil in a large skillet over medium heat. Add the onions and sauté until soft, about 5 minutes. Stir in the garlic and cook another 30 seconds. Remove from heat.

Place the cooked onions and garlic in a food processor along with the tofu, salt, pepper, lemon juice and basil. Pulse until just combined. You want it to be similar in texture to ricotta—creamy but not pureed. Season to taste, if needed.

"FRESH" TOMATO SAUCE

— MAKES ABOUT 3½ CUPS (828 ML) —

For pasta in a hurry, try this "fresh" tomato sauce using canned tomatoes. It's bright, flavorful and healthy. Place a pot of water on for pasta at the same time you start the sauce. When the pasta is done cooking, the sauce should be ready! I'm including a tablespoon (15 g) of butter to be stirred in at the end of the dish. I know it's tempting to skip this step, but it really elevates the basic, canned sauce by creating a silky texture that coats every noodle.

1 tsp extra virgin olive oil

½ white or yellow onion, chopped

3 cloves garlic, minced

1 (28-oz [795-g]) can petite diced tomatoes in juice

¼ tsp crushed red pepper flakes, or more for a spicy kick

Salt and freshly ground black pepper

1 tbsp (15 g) butter

1 cup (25 g) fresh basil, chopped

Heat olive oil in a medium saucepan over medium heat. Add in the onion and garlic and cook, stirring often, until soft, about 5 minutes. Stir in the tomatoes and juice, crushed red pepper flakes, salt and pepper and simmer for 15–20 minutes while pasta cooks.

Just before serving, remove from heat and stir in 1 tablespoon (15 g) butter and basil. Season to taste and serve over hot pasta.

VEGAN VERSION: Replace butter with dairy-free butter, same amount.

PROTEIN-PACKED PESTO

— MAKES ABOUT 2 CUPS (480 G) —

I adore fresh pesto. And really, who doesn't? It's basically a mixture of three delicious fats—olive oil, cheese and pine nuts—mixed with fresh herbs. It should come as no surprise that I love it, especially when my basil plant is overflowing come midsummer. I would eat pesto every day on everything if I didn't feel like I was spooning oil into my mouth with each bite. Enter this protein-packed pesto! Using white beans creates a creamy, herb-based sauce that's great on pasta or spread on a sandwich. It's a bit thicker than traditional pesto, so toss with reserved pasta water and hot pasta to thin. To cut down on costs, I'm using walnuts instead of pine nuts, but feel free to swap in your favorite nut or seed.

3 large bunches basil, about 1–1½ cups (24–36 g) packed basil leaves

2 cloves garlic

2 tbsp (10 g) nutritional yeast

1 cup (55 g) cannellini beans

½ cup (65 g) walnuts

2 tbsp (30 ml) water, preferably pasta water if you're making this to go with pasta

½ tbsp (8 ml) white wine vinegar or fresh lemon juice

Salt and freshly ground black pepper

2 tbsp (30 ml) extra virgin olive oil

Put all of the ingredients except olive oil in a food processor. Coarsely chop until the mixture looks like fine meal. With the blade running, pour in the olive oil and continue to process for about 1 minute until smooth. If the sauce is too thick, slowly add more water.

ROASTED TOMATO SAUCE

— MAKES ABOUT 1½ CUPS (355 ML) —

This is how I make "fresh" tomato sauce in the winter. A long roast of cherry tomatoes lets their flavor slowly concentrate into a chunky sauce. If you make this in the summer, any combination of tomatoes will do, but I tend to favor this one in the months where it's almost impossible to find a juicy, fresh tomato. Incredible over penne, this roasted sauce also tastes great alongside my favorite appetizer: top toasted crostini with whipped ricotta cheese, roasted cherry tomatoes, a drizzle of balsamic reduction and fresh basil leaves.

16 oz (455 g) cherry tomatoes

1 tbsp (15 ml) extra virgin olive oil

3 large cloves garlic, chopped

Salt and freshly ground black pepper

Preheat oven to 400°F (204°C). Toss together the cherry tomatoes, olive oil, garlic and a pinch each of salt and pepper and place in a glass baking dish.

Cook for 30 minutes, stirring halfway through, until most of the tomatoes have burst. Remove from heat and toss the tomatoes and juices with cooked penne pasta.

For a delicious appetizer, toast crostini and spread with whipped ricotta. Pile on the roasted tomatoes and garnish with balsamic reduction and fresh basil leaves.

the italian pantry

Ironically, in our century-old home, I don't even have a pantry. My current Italian pantry is made up of spices overflowing the cupboards, canned goods in half of the buffet and an excess of pasta, pots and pans tucked neatly away in the basement. An amusing situation, but a small sacrifice to live in a home with so much character.

Regardless of your individual kitchen setup, stocking the right ingredients makes it so much easier to create healthy, balanced meals. I make it a point to always have a few boxes of pasta (preferably whole wheat), cans of beans, lentils, extra virgin olive oil, dried herbs, spices and cans of tomato products in my pantry. These items, combined with fresh produce, are the base for a majority of my meals. Living in an older home without a pantry is a nice reminder that you don't have to stock a thousand ingredients in order to be a good cook.

For me, "maximum flavor with minimal effort" means eating produce with the seasons. If you've ever had a watery, flavorless tomato in January, you know the difference that a few months can make. Even though most produce is available year-round, limiting my ingredients to what's in-season is a big component of me creating simple, delicious food. A rustic dish of fresh tomatoes, basil and penne is incredible in August but lackluster in February. When you're working in harmony with nature, it's much easier to produce yummy, mouthwatering food.

Finally, cooking doesn't have to be complicated. The majority of the recipes in this book are designed to increase your cooking confidence. To help, I've included a section of my best tips and tricks to help you produce dishes your family will love. Being fearless in the kitchen comes from cooking often. Cooking tips aside, you can only build confidence in the kitchen by actually being in the kitchen. So get in there, break a dish or two and have fun.

PASTA COOKING TIPS

Always cook pasta in a large pot with generously salted water. Using a big-enough pot will allow the pasta to swim freely, cooking evenly and releasing their starches.

Salting the water beforehand allows the pasta to absorb the salt while it's cooking, reducing the need for additional salt in the dish. It's why I use the term "salt, to taste" in most of my pasta dishes. If the pasta is properly seasoned while cooking, you don't need much additional salt in the final dish.

Before draining the pasta, I always reserve a quarter cup (59 ml) to a half cup (118 ml) of pasta cooking water. The easiest way to do this is to ladle the pasta into a cup before draining, so as not to burn yourself. I almost always add a little reserved pasta water to my sauce, as it helps to loosen the sauce and adds starch, which allows the sauce to cling to the pasta.

Don't add olive oil to the water! I'm not sure where this tip came from, but save your olive oil for dressing. As long as you have a large-enough pot for the pasta to swim in, you don't have to worry about it clumping together.

In a similar fashion, once the pasta is drained, don't coat it with olive oil to prevent sticking. This will inhibit sauce from clinging to the pasta and add additional calories and fat.

Don't rinse cooked pasta! Rinsing pasta removes the starch on the surface, which helps the sauce adhere to the noodle. The only exception to this rule is if the pasta will be used in a cold salad, in which case you do rinse the noodles.

Cook the pasta until just al dente, and no longer. I would rather my pasta be slightly undercooked then mushy and gummy. To do this, I typically set a timer to test the pasta a minute or two before the recommended cooking time on the package. Al dente pasta should have a little bite to it, without being pasty white or hard inside.

THE ITALIAN PANTRY

In addition to fresh vegetables and plenty of onion and garlic, these are the staples that make meals easy and effortless.

DRIED HERBS AND SPICES

I know it's tempting to purchase cheaper versions of dried herbs and spices, but high-quality herbs and spices are a small way to amplify your cooking. You should replace your spices every six months, or at least every year. Old spices lose their potency and can actually ruin your meal instead of enhance it. I suggest buying dried herbs and spices from the bulk bin whenever possible, to ensure that you're only getting as much as you need at one time. Not only does this save you money, you also get to experiment with lots of flavors without investing in larger packages.

I use dried thyme, dried oregano, crushed red pepper flakes, black peppercorns in a pepper mill (for freshly ground black pepper), dried basil and dried rosemary almost daily.

BEANS AND LEGUMES

Canned beans are a great shortcut; just make sure to drain and rinse the beans before using, unless directed otherwise. If I have the time, I like to buy dry beans to pressure-cook in large batches. From there, I freeze whatever I don't use in individual-sized portions. My favorite beans/legumes are chickpeas, white beans and lentils.

GRAINS

Quinoa, brown rice, arborio rice, ground polenta (cornmeal) and farro are my most-loved grains.

PASTA AND NOODLES

I probably have a larger dried pasta section in my pantry than most. A variety of noodles will provide endless meal options. I like to have at least one box of long (linguine or spaghetti), short (rigatoni or penne), small (macaroni or shells) and a soup (ditalini or orzo) pasta on hand. While whole-wheat options are best for added nutrients and fiber, it's okay if you can only find the white-flour version. As long as you are adding plenty of vegetables (like most of the recipes here), you will benefit from the extra vitamins, minerals and fiber without the use of whole-wheat pasta. Brands of dried pasta do matter. My favorites are Barilla and DeLallo. Dreamfields makes an excellent whole-grain pasta.

NUTS AND SEEDS

I'm fascinated by Dan Buettner's research on the Blue Zones. Blue Zones are areas of the world where people not only live the longest, but also have the highest numbers of people reaching 100. Researchers examined their habits and compared them across regions. For the most part, those who live in Blue Zones follow a high-vegetarian, high-carb diet. Roughly 65 percent of their diet is whole grains, beans and starchy tubers, and their snack of choice is nuts. Sounds just like the Italian diet, doesn't it? Because of the health benefits of nuts, I like to include them as a nice crunch on salads and pasta dishes. I use them as a base in my Vegan Parmesan Cheese (page 182), and puree them for silky, dairy-free sauces like my cashew cream. While I love all nuts, I turn to walnuts, cashews and almonds most frequently, though pine nuts are an indulgent treat every now and then.

CANNED GOODS

I use a lot of canned tomato products in my recipes for both ease and convenience. My pantry is stocked with cans of diced tomatoes, crushed tomatoes and whole tomatoes. My favorite brands include Hunt's, Muir Glen, Pomì and Cento's San Marzano tomato products.

OILS

I always have on hand at least two different types of olive oil: unrefined extra virgin for salad dressings and finishing dishes and olive oil for cooking. While you don't need to spend a fortune on olive oils, in general the more expensive the oil, the better tasting it will be. Skip the $5 jugs of olive oil at the grocery store and go for something with more taste and body.

VINEGARS

Here's a secret to becoming a better cook; add a little bit of acid. Most savory dishes benefit from a bit of acid, whether it's red wine vinegar, lemon juice or a yummy balsamic. If a dish has enough salt and still tastes flat, it's often because it's missing that burst of acidity. I rely on red wine vinegar, balsamic vinegar and lemon juice most often to add a pinch of brightness to a finished dish. If you end up adding too much acid, mute the sourness with fat or sugar.

PARMESAN CHEESE

If you haven't noticed by now, I end most of my dishes with a generous sprinkle of grated Parmesan cheese. Its savory, salty bite enhances the flavor and texture of even the most basic dish. However, most Parmesan cheese isn't technically vegetarian. Most imported Parmesans contain animal rennet, an enzyme that helps separate milk into curds and whey. According to European Union law, it cannot be labeled Parmesan unless it contains milk, salt and animal rennet. I prefer to choose domestic Parmesan cheeses made with vegetable rennet or microbial rennet instead of the animal counterpart. My favorite animal-rennet-free Parmesans are: Organic Valley Shredded Parmesan Cheese, Whole Foods' 365 Vegetarian Grated Parmesan, Trader Joe's Grated Parmesan and Shredded Parmesan and BelGioioso Vegetarian Parmesan wedge, perfect for grate-it-yourself.

PASTA MIX AND MATCH

While the flavor of pasta doesn't vary much from strand to tube, the shape of the various pastas makes a big difference to the overall finished dish. Here's a quick overview of basic pasta shapes and what sauces they pair best with.

PENNE: Perhaps my favorite shape, this short, hollow pasta is widely available in both whole-wheat and gluten-free varieties. Penne is best used in salads, baked pastas and with thicker sauces so the ingredients can get inside of the pasta tube.

RIGATONI: Wider than penne, rigatoni is best paired with chunky sauces like a Bolognese or mushroom sauce. The ridges make it ideal for heartier sauces to cling to.

LINGUINE: A long, flat noodle that pairs well with silky, sturdy sauces. Tomato, pesto or a light cream sauce works best.

SPAGHETTI: Is there anything better than twirling spaghetti noodles? It pairs nicely with simple sauces like tomato, cacio e pepe (cheese and black pepper) and puttanesca.

CAPELLINI (ANGEL HAIR PASTA): Long, thin noodles that go best with sauces that won't weigh them down. Try with a simple coating of olive oil and minced garlic or a light tomato-basil sauce.

BOW TIES (FARFALLE): This is my favorite shape for cheese-based sauces or any pasta dish that I serve to kids. I love their fun butterfly shape—it always puts a smile on my face!

ELBOWS: This noodle is a classic for mac and cheese and works well in pasta salads. For a fun twist on traditional macaroni and cheese, try it with small shells!

ORZO: This might be my husband's favorite, a tiny, rice-shaped pasta that's perfect in soup and salads. Or you can enjoy it the way my two-year-old niece does, with a little olive oil, salt and pepper and plenty of freshly grated Parmesan cheese.

PERFECT PASTA PORTIONS

When you cook pasta, two ounces (55 g) of dry pasta per portion is a good rule to follow. Of course, unless you have a scale, two ounces (55 g) of pasta can be difficult to measure. Use the chart below to create perfect portions of pasta every time.

PASTA SHAPE	DRY PASTA — 2-OZ (55-G) SERVING	COOKED PASTA — CUPS (GRAMS)
Capellini (angel hair)	2.125" (5.5 cm) circumference	1 cup
Fettuccine	2.125" (5.5 cm) circumference	1 cup
Linguine	2.125" (5.5 cm) circumference	1 cup
Spaghetti	2.125" (5.5 cm) circumference	1 cup
Elbows	½ cup (55 g)	1⅛ cups
Bow Ties (farfalle)	¾ cup (55 g)	1¼ cups
Gemelli	½ cup (55 g)	1⅛ cups
Rigatoni	¾ cup (55 g)	1¼ cups
Penne	⅔ cup (55 g)	1¼ cups
Mezze Penne (small penne)	½ cup (55 g)	1 cup
Rotini	½ cup (55 g)	1 cup
Ziti	⅔ cup (55 g)	1¼ cups
Orzo	¼ cup (55 g)	⅔ cup
Orecchiette	½ cup (55 g)	¾ cup
Bucatini	2¾" (7 cm) circumference	1½ cups
Ditalini	⅓ cup (55 g)	1¼ cups
Gnocchi	½ cup (55 g)	¾ cup
Pastina	⅓ cup (55 g)	1¼ cups
Pennette	½ cup (55 g)	1 cup
Large Shells	¾ cup (55 g)	1¼ cups

acknowledgments

I've dreamed of crafting an Italian cookbook for ages; the notion that it's actually in print is incredibly humbling and gratifying. There are so many wonderful people who have poured their time and energy into supporting this passion project, to whom I am forever grateful.

TO MY HUSBAND, BRYAN: I don't know how to put into words how much I appreciate the support and love you give me. Thank you for washing the dishes, eating pasta for months on end without complaint, wiping away my frustrated tears and being my biggest cheerleader. Without question, you are my better half and my best friend. MFEO.

TO MY MOM, BARBARA: Thank you for igniting my love of food and for the countless hours of conversation around menus, ingredients and "what are we going to make next?" exchanges. I am grateful for your kindness, words of encouragement and selfless love. Thanks for giving so much of you so that I can be who I am today.

TO LOU AND KATMANDO, MY SOUS CHEFS: Thanks for always being game to try my crazy concoctions. Mada-pasta forever.

TO DAD AND THE ENTIRE CASPERO/CANNON/LENZ CLAN: Thanks for your enthusiasm and love.

TO CHERI: Thank you for your magical editing powers; your feedback is always so thoughtful.

TO MARISSA, WILL AND EVERYONE AT PAGE STREET: Thanks for believing in me.

TO JENNIFER BLUME: Thanks for making my creations come to life.

LASTLY, THANK YOU TO MY RECIPE TESTERS: Mariel Abbitt, Katherin Abrams, Allison Baltzer, Kendra Bruno, Kosti Efstathiou, Sara Haas, Kira Hogan, Allison Huebner, Arnie Kahn, Katie Kelly, Katie Kratz, Paula Lenz, Ashley Lovich, Kara Minnich, Laurie Reda, Carly Rowland, Caitlin Sommers and Laura Yanez. Because of you, I am confident in every recipe between these pages. Thank you for your edits, your feedback and your time.

about the author

 Alexandra Caspero Lenz, MA, R.D., RYT, is a registered dietitian and nutrition expert with a passion for both health and wellness. A nationally recognized nutritionist, she has been featured in *Food Network Magazine, Forbes, Details, Vogue, Men's Health* and other publications. Her blog, Delish Knowledge, focuses on making whole-food vegetarian eating deliciously simple. She lives in St. Louis, Missouri, with her husband Bryan.

index